Oxford to Cambridge Railway in Profile

Volume 1
Oxford - Bletchley

by
Bill Simpson

Lamplight Publications

Lamplight Publications

260 Colwell Drive, Witney, Oxon OX28 5LW

First published 2006

© Lamplight Publications and Bill Simpson

All rights reserved
No part of this book may be reproduced, stored in
a retrieval system or transmitted in
any form or by means electronic, mechanical,
photocopying, recording or otherwise without
prior approval of the publishers

ISBN 978 1 899246 16 8

Designed and typeset by Lamplight Publications
Printed and bound by the Alden Press

Claydon station looking towards Verney Junction and Bletchley on May 18, 1959

F A Blencowe

Chapters

Oxford 9

Islip 29

Bicester 33

Launton. 43

Marsh Gibbon 47

Claydon 51

Verney Junction 57

Winslow. 63

Swanbourne 69

Bletchley 73

Rewley Road - The Model. 85

Acknowledgements

The author would like to convey his thanks to the following. Andrew Bratton of the Buckinghamshire Railway Centre, R M Casserley, Ron White of Colour-Rail, The Oxford Model Railway Club, LNWR Society, All of the photographers that have so generously allowed photographs from their collections to be used are acknowledged beneath their photographs.

Front cover, background illustration of Swanbourne station in 1984. *Bill Simpson*

Inset, two LNWR engines c1920, 'Renown' class 1936 *Royal Sovereign* piloting a 'Precedent' class no 1166 *Wyre* passing Port Meadow Halt. Significantly the train has three horseboxes. *L&GRP*

Back cover illustration of a 'Prince of Wales' class *Falaba* that became LMS 25683 at Bletchley platform no 2 in 1938 with an Oxford train. *Colour-Rail*

A former Midland class 3P 4-4-0 no. 762 on the Oxford LMS turntable just prior to World War Two. Introduced 1901 twenty-two of these engines survived nationalisation but were soon reduced to eighteen and all had gone by 1952. The Oxford-Cambridge line was one of the routes upon which they worked out their twilight years.

George Hine

The view over Islip crossing looking towards Oxford.

Introduction

The railway from Oxford to Cambridge was born out of territorial protractions of new railways in the nineteenth century.

In 1834 the London & Birmingham Railway built its great trunk line north and opened it in 1838.

Another railway, the Great Western Railway, proceeded from London west to Bristol in 1835. Between them was a huge section of the country from the Thames Valley to the west Midlands that was certain to be drawn into the net of one or both of these companies as towns made demands for extended branches.

The London & Birmingham were developing Rugby and the people of Aylesbury wanted a branch to pass through their town and go to Oxford in 1839-40. In the event Aylesbury remained a terminus and Oxford was connected by a branch to the GWR in 1844. Who were also poised to go north of there with a scheme to go to Rugby (Oxford & Rugby Railway) and another to go to Worcester and Wolverhampton (Oxford, Worcester & Wolverhampton Railway). The London & Birmingham became alarmed and proposed lines to counter the GWR from near Harrow north to Buckingham and through Banbury (The London, Worcester & South Staffordshire Railway). After a period of litigious conflict the GWR carried the day, not to Rugby, but to Birmingham, which left a wide area still without railways. Two schemes left high and dry amongst this conflicting web of proposed lines were the Buckingham and Brackley Junction Railway and the Oxford & Bletchley Railway. These were supported by Sir Harry Verney of Claydon and the Marquess of Chandos, later Duke of Buckingham.

The L&B as a result of some political manoeuvering became part of a great amalgam called the London & North Western Railway. This company supported the continuation of these schemes amalgamated as the Buckinghamshire Railway, extended further from Brackley to Banbury. They still harboured the potential for moving north of Banbury. So much so that they opened the line to Banbury in May 1850 from a crossing point of the main line near Fenny Stratford. This came to be the township of Bletchley. At a point near Claydon the line devided with a fork going to Oxford opening in May 1851.

A Bedford Railway had earlier been very quick off the mark with a line from the same point at Bletchley to Bedford. It was intended to be equally vigorous in continuing this to the city of Cambridge with the help of the Eastern Counties Railway. Unfortunately due to a railway scandal concerning one George Hudson, one of the leading board members of the ECR, a crisis forestalled the

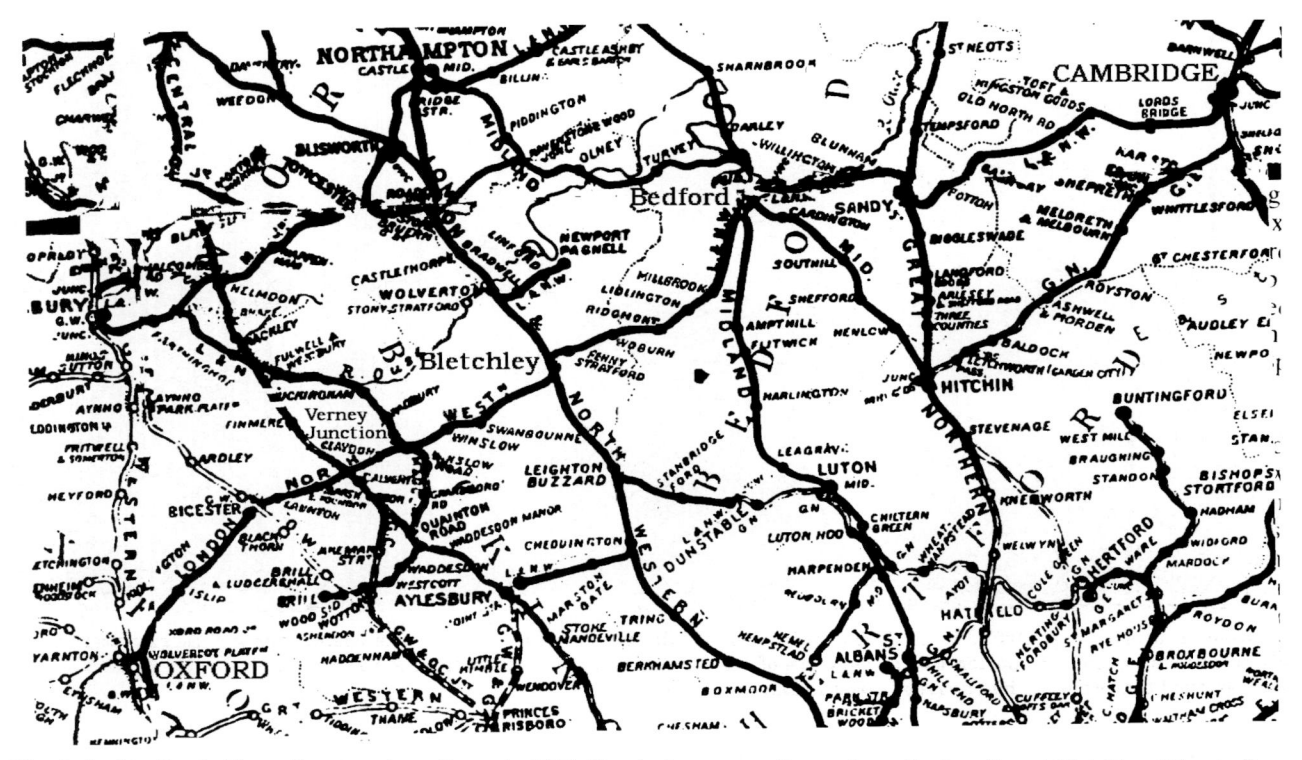

The Oxford to Cambridge railway route as it was in 1921. Few trains ran continuously as the junction at Bletchley did not allow this without crossing and interrupting the main line services. Consequently Bletchley was much used as a change station.
Bill Simpson Collection

The former LNWR/LMS station as coal yard sidings at Oxford in the late 1950s with ex-GWR 2-6-2 'Prairie' tank engine. Palls of drifting steam and the coal gritted yard presents the railway atmosphere of fifty years ago beneath the spire of Nuffield College.
Laurence Waters

The front of the station at Oxford in 1935. The enticement of railway travel to reach places of leisure was well represented in this decade with exemplery poster designs as works of art. The LMS particularly triumphed the contemplative Lake District. The GWR extolled that England had a riviera coast in Devon and Cornwall.

Entrance to the goods yard at Oxford in 1935. The approach road to the GWR station is on the left. On such a cheerless day the refreshment cabin on the right would no doubt find good custom. It was for such a long time a feature, between the two stations, used much by bus and taxi drivers.

Bedford - Cambridge line. After many frustrated attempts to retrieve the situation a line was finally built and opened in 1862. At last there was a cross-country line between the two famous cities of academia. Much to the point was the fact that nearly every main line and succeeding main line radiating north from London could be accessed. The GWR to Bristol and the west at Oxford; the GWR line from Paddington to Birmingham at Bicester (1910); the Metropolitan Railway (1894) and Great Central Railway (1899) via Verney Junction to Aylesbury; the main line at Bletchley (1838); the Midland main line at Bedford (1857), (1868); the Great Northern Railway (1851). With the Great Eastern Railway at Cambridge. The only exception being the GER main line to Colchester,

The route continued to be run successfully throughout the nineteenth century and for the first three decades of the twentieth.

As the LNWR passed into the ownership

A D16 4-4-0 approaching Oxford Road Junction in September 1959 with a train to Oxford from Cambridge. Note the mineral wagons and coal staithes on the siding installed in 1850 for such a purpose.

J D Edwards

of the London, Midland & Scottish Railway, an even greater almagam, it sought to find economies. One was passing much control of their station at Oxford to the GWR.

The route found a very important role during World War Two when it carried a lot of traffic around London by the construction of a number of freight link-up lines.

After that war the railways entered a parlous state of war wear and became nationalised under the name of British Ralways, part of the Brtish Transport Commission. With the drift of all traffic towards the new developing road system BR considered the railway serously under-used with higher terminal costs like track and signalling and the manning of many under-used stations.

Consequently the Board of Trade appointed a Doctor Richard Beeching, a board member of ICI to oversee and report on the railways. The findings and conclusions of the report and the subsequent enactment of its findings is a much chronicled period of railway history. Interestingly Dr Beeching was largely in favour of the Oxbridge line and its potential as a freight diversionary route, nevertheless in the later Beeching period it was decided that the line was a liability.

Closure notices were posted for the last day of 1967. The line between Bletchley and Bedford literally hung on by its teeth as a successful bus replacement could not be cobbled together.

The line from Bedford to Cambridge seemed inexorably doomed along with the Oxford - Bletchley, although the latter crucially managed to keep the track in use for freight. A section of it is rusting at the present time but it still retains the opportunity of being reinstated.

New housing in Milton Keynes and Aylesbury has given a new impetus to the prospect of a rail link-up between the two towns. The case for travelling by rail is picking up momentum all the time as more and more people feel their time being wasted sitting in traffic jams. The problem is how the railways will meet that demand.

The progress and development of Chiltern Railways with commodious car parks and supplying a country bus service is most impressive and it has met an enthusiastic response.

If the Milton Keynes - Aylesbury service is also extended to Oxford it would effectively bring back two thirds of the connection to Cambridge. The prospects for restoring the route entire seem tenuous and uncertain to say the least.

Oxford in the 1930s with a train entering hauled by one of the LNWR 5ft 6in 2-4-2 tanks. A bit too grimy to make out the number, Bletchley had a group of these for working the cross country route and branches. Note the station sign of the LNWR style with white letters on a dark blue ground.

R M Casserley Collection

Oxford

The LNWR line to Oxford always fought against the disadvantage of distance after the building of the GWR line from Princes Risborough to Oxford (1864) which made Paddington 55¾ miles away. By the old route via Didcot it is 65½ miles. From Euston to Oxford via Bletchley was a significant 78 miles with a change at Bletchley. Consequently the line was seen mostly as a cross-country route connecting with nearly all the main lines out of London north of the capital, with the exception of the Great Eastern Railway line via Colchester.

In the 1930s the London Midland & Scottish Railway, recovering from the great amalgamation of 1923, was looking, as most large undertakings do, to reducing their costs by pooling resources. The competitive conflicts of the pregrouping companies were no longer a central issue. This massive conglomerate required great organising ability to run it successfully.

The upshot of this was that the LMS at Oxford were keen to hand over the running of much of their Oxford station to the GWR that was situated alongside. In 1935 by an Act of Parliament the LMS handed over the responsibility of the swingbridge at the entrance to the station, crossing the link channel between the Oxford Canal and the River Isis, to the GWR. Maintenance of this was crucial to operating the entire station. The canal was still being made considerable use of and great deal of the Oxford city coal supplies passed over that bridge into the sidings. In 1934 the Stationmaster of the GWR took over responsibility of the LMS station.

The line to Bletchley was still part of the LMS system and later British Railways Midland Region until 1951 when part of it was ceded to Western Region with a boundary marker between Bicester and Launton on the 18 mp.

The second world war developed further the gradual absorption of the Oxford LMS to

Oxford British Railways Midland Region in 1949. It appears that the glazing has been removed on the Porte cochere and in the author's experience this is the last photograph seen before an early 1950s view by which time a considerable portion of the front had been removed. The reasons for the removal remain a mystery and all that can be deduced is that at least some of it now resides in store with the Science Museum.

R M Casserley Collection

The view in 1919 from the platform looking into the train shed. The buildings on the distant left existed before the Rewley Road was cut through alongside the station. The considerable combined goods shed on the right came about by an agreement between the OWW and LNWR. This was made during the days of the former's transgression from the GWR whereby it gained access to Oxford. In the foreground is one of the beautiful 'bell-jar' type LNWR gaslights with the station name etched on the glass.

L&GRP

A superbly panoramic view is created by joining two photographs of an elevated view. It provides a wealth of detail with the GWR timber shed on the left, auto coach visible for working the branches. On the right is the former LNWR shed area with Standard locomotive type in the shed and Stanier 8F alongside it. Between them is the one time siding connection that existed up until the second world war when a new double track junction was built further north. Likely date of photograph would be very early 1950s with a Riddles engine being present and just before the roof profile was altered on St Barnabas's Church.

Lens of Sutton

the GWR. This took the form of a proper double track junction north between the 30 and 31 mile junction mileposts. This was opened in November 1940. It seems incredible that all through an age that depended very much on the railways that the two railway companies were still connected only by an exchange siding north of the swingbridge.

The new double track junction ensured that traffic could move on a wartime ring of railways around London to avoid congestion on bombed out lines. It proved to be a considerable advantage at Oxford and many trains hauled by imported United States locomotives ran freight over the line.

It was now possible for trains from Cambridge to run straight into a bay of the GWR station and for goods trains to run through Oxford south to Hinksey yard. This meant also that LMS engines would go onto the GWR loco steam shed which had a longer turntable.

Nationalisation of the railways in 1948 continued the amalgamation and the former LNWR/LMS station ceased passenger operation in 1951.

The steam shed was closed in 1950.

This was a final flourish of the Bletchley line which ran on in full service until the last day of 1967.

The station site was still used for coal deliveries and apparently beer. The former continued until the late 1980s.

The station building remained in an indecisive limbo for a number of years whilst various schemes of development and redesigning the road junction in front of the station were pondered and negotiated.

Finally in 1998 all the interested parties concluded funding arrangements and the historic building was moved, not without spectacular publicity. It was restored and re-erected successfully at the Buckinghamshire Railway centre at Quainton.

The site was then developed and is now the location of the Said Business School.

The line to Bicester was reopened in 1987 and has continued although there have been attempts to reduce the service.

The view of the station front as a tyre depot in April 1970 with the Port cochere removed. When the building was found a new home at the Buckinghamshire Railway Centre the known original appearance was restored.

H C Casserley

One of the resourceful little LNWR 2-4-0's collectively known as 'Jumbos' at Rewley Road in January 1925. The now preserved famous 'Hardwick' of this group worked on the Oxford - Cambridge route at this time.

LNWR Society

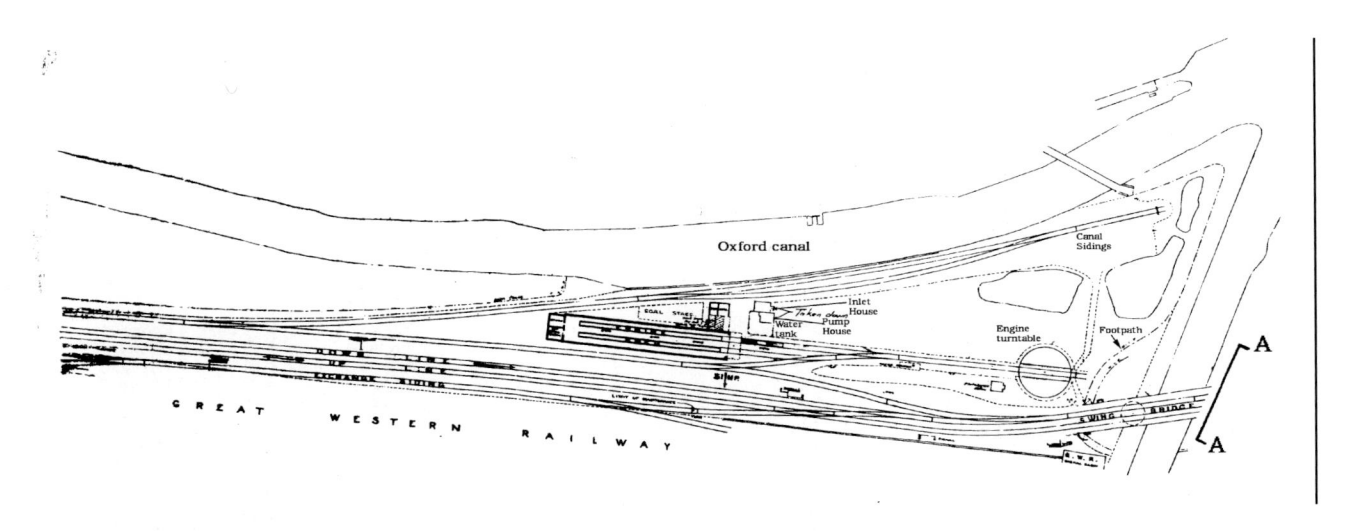

The shed area and the bridge over the 'Sheepwash Channel'. Note the modest siding connection between the LNWR and the GWR.

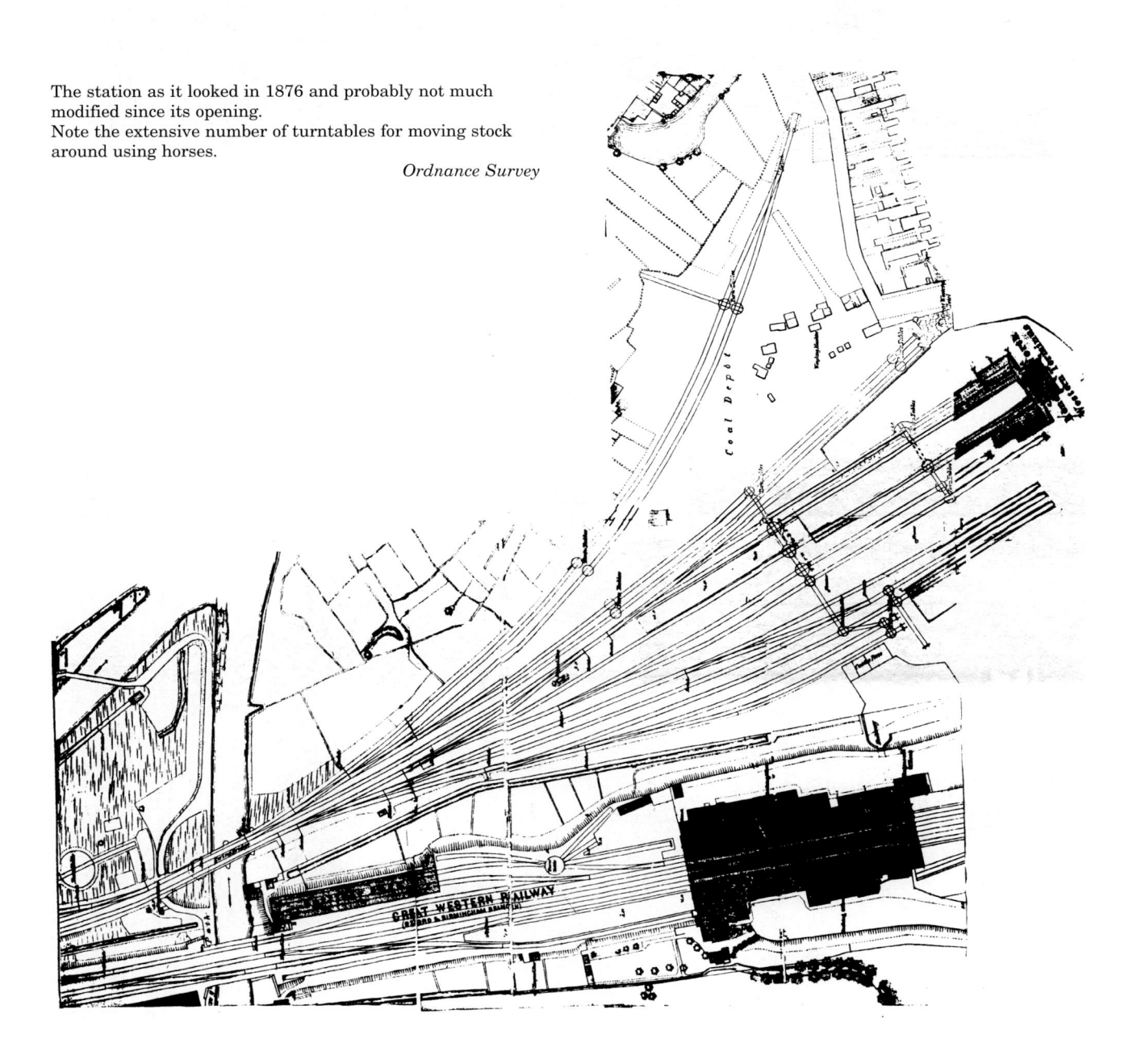

The station as it looked in 1876 and probably not much modified since its opening.
Note the extensive number of turntables for moving stock around using horses.

Ordnance Survey

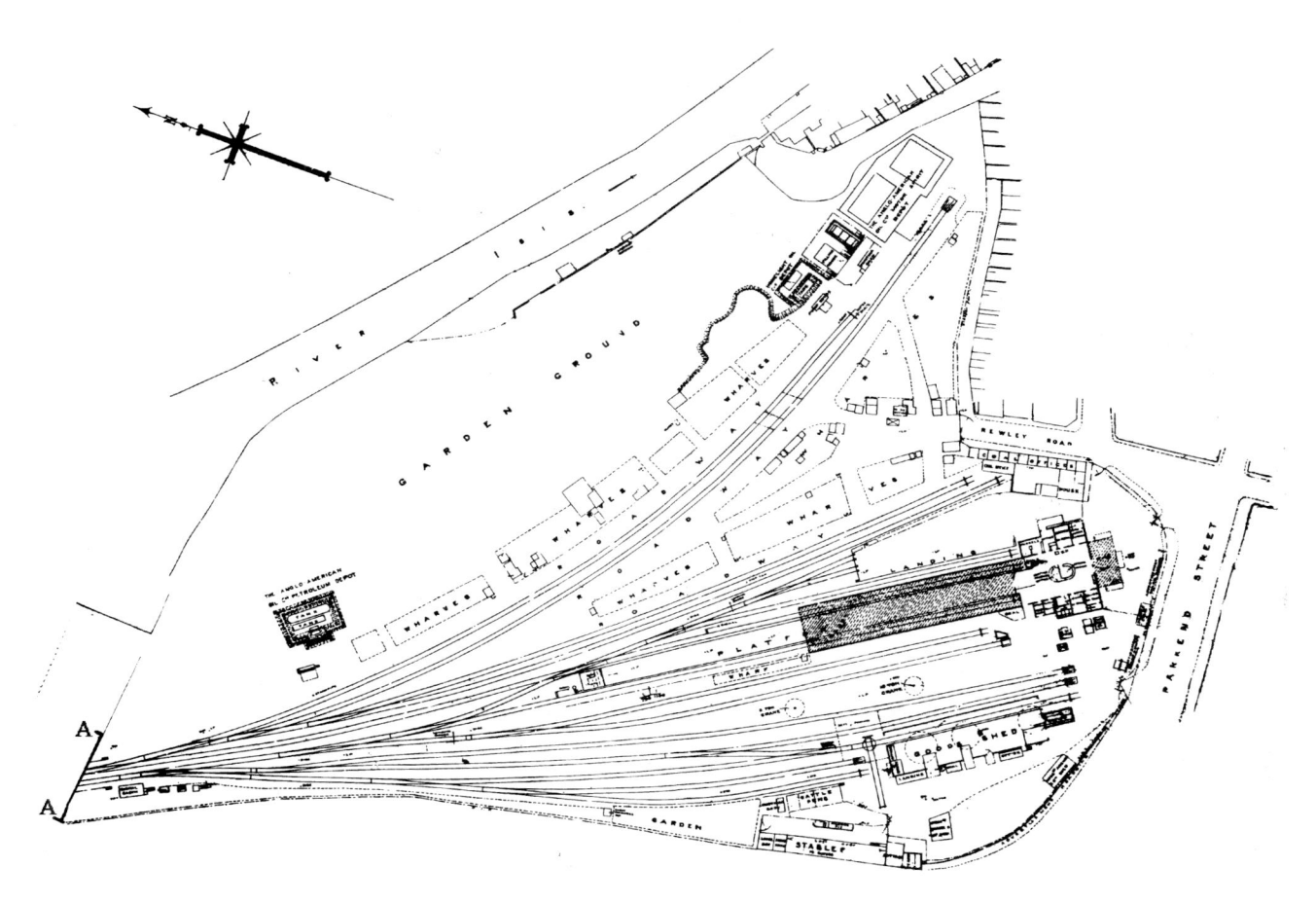

The station area at Oxford in the 1920's after it had become part of the LMS network. The station reached over quite a wide area with the stops for the coal siding not far from the canal bridge on Hythe Bridge Street.

The coal offices on Rewley Road in the early 1980's. Much of the city's coal was transacted through these offices.

Bill Simpson

An 0-8-0 'Super D' type steam locomotive with brake van trundles across the very remarkable swingbridge in the 1960s. As the front is pointing in the right direction for a return to Bletchley it has presumably been over to the GWR to turn round and may be about to find a return working diagram.

Oxford MRC Collection

With occasional use of the coal yard it became a rarity to see the bridge in position across the 'Sheepwash Channel' as in the 1980s when this photograph was taken. Although the footpath is still available the area has been considerably built up with housing to the point where the bridge seems to be an anachronistic intrusion.

Bill Simpson

Impressive motive power of the former LNWR in the 1930s under the ownership of the LMS standing near the exchange siding. All 4-6-0 types, the first locomotive is a '19 inch Goods' original number 1565 now numbered LMS 8813, this was withdrawn in 1934. The second locomotive is also a '19 inch Goods' original number 1368, now numbered 8828 withdrawn in 1935. Behind are two unidentifiable 'Prince of Wales' class.

Oxford MRC Collection

An interesting view looking north across the bridge showing the proximity of both the GWR and LNWR signalboxes in the 1950s. The LNWR box did not see out that decade and is obviously derelict in this photgraph, the GWR box remained until 1973.

Oxford MRC Collection

A Webb Coal Tank crossing the swingbridge no 7733. This engine was introduced in April 1886 as no 2457, not only taking its LMS number but also British Railways no 58907 before its withdrawal in September 1948.

Oxford MRC Collection

A sad decline. The view of the shed area after all working had been transferred to the GWR. It seems now so regrettable that such a unique structure as the water tower intergrating a building pattern of castings from the Great Exhibition of 1851 was simply thrown to scrap.

Lens of Sutton

The view looking back towards the station with the bridge open for the canal. Note the forground pathway across the rails, this would allow the canal boatmen to walk their horses across the line.

Oxford Model Railway Club Collection

On the original canal siding lines that became part of the locomotive stem shed two LNWR engines in 1926. An 0-8-0 no 1844 which is a Webb 'A' class 3-cylinder compound. This engine was introduced in 1898, renumbered LMS no 8985 in January 1927; it was withdrawn in 1930. The other engine is one of the 0-6-0 saddletanks that shunted the station area. The LMS wagon is for loco coal and freshly painted proclaiming the new ownership.

Mr R Abbot

A local train approaching the station alongside the steam shed hauled by one of the LNWR 2-4-2 5ft 6in tank engines under the bracket signals of the original LNWR. Note the line leading to the exchange siding on the left.

Oxford MRC Collection

One of the LNWR 'George V' class no 1777 'Widgeon' on Oxford shed. It was issued with LMS number 5378 which it took in October 1927, that would obviously place this view prior to then.

Oxford MRC Collection

A GWR utilisation of the shed lines in the 1930s. In 1934 the GWR Stationmaster took over administration of the former LNWR/LMS station. If therefore the GWR turntable was pressed with a queue of too many engines the Churchward 2-6-0's would be able to use the restricted LNWR turntable which may be what is happening.

Oxford Model Railway Club Collection

One of the '19 inch Goods' class no 8869 on the Oxford LNWR turntable. Originally numbered 1770 as new in 1909. It took this number in 1926 and was fitted with a Belpaire firebox. It was withdrawn in November 1935. Note the verty tight restriction of the turntable for the 4-6-0.

Oxford MRC Collection

21

The one occasion when the Oxford shed could play host to an engine seldom seen south of Birmingham, a Lanacashire & Yorkshire Railway 4-6-0 N1 class 5P 4-cylinder loco. The class started life as a massive 4-6-4 'Baltic' tank but only ten were built as such and further building was to the profile seen here. They continued to number 70 of a class but started to be withdrawn from 1934 onwards. A mere seven lasted into British Railways ownership and the last, no 10455, went in 1951. As a Hughes engine one easily see the similarities of the much more successful Hughes/Fowler 2-6-0 'Crab'. If the engine was turned at Oxford it would have to had to have been on the GWR turntable, or labouriously by being detatched from the tender which was done on some occasions.

Oxford MRC Collection

It was tough employment for railwaymen during the age of steam. After a long shift shovelling a fair proportion of the contents of the tender into the firebox the crew could be required to turn the engine for its next working as can be seen here. The loco is an 0-8-0 no 1874 'A' three-cylinder Compound introduced in 1900. It became LMS 9054 in July 1926, then was re-classified G1 in 1928 and survived to become British Railways 49054 before being withdrawn in April 1949.

Mr R Abbot

Looking rather forlorn one of the Webb modified original Ramsbottom 0-6-0 Saddletanks No 3610 at the shed in the 1930's. These 'Special' tanks were introduced in 1870 and totalled 260; they were used at large stations from Euston north for moving stock around. The cab roof was added by Webb.

Mr R Abbot

One of the Webb 'Coal Tanks' no 7733, originally LNWR no 2457 introduced in April 1886. The locomotive was allocated number 58907 by British Railways but as this was in September 1948 it is unlikely that it carried the number. They were used extensively from Bletchley shed and their steady but unremarkable progress meant that they were useful for branch line work. Consequently they were used on the Banbury, Newport Pagnell, Dunstable and Aylesbury branches.

Oxford MRC Collection

In 1932 the Micheline Tyre Company of France were involved in an experimental railbus with flanged rubber tyres. They convinced the LMS to have trials on the selected Oxford - Bletchley line. This kind of thing had begun in the early days of the century with steam railmotors. It was the continuing struggle to reconcile operating costs to payload more economically, especially on branch or secondary lines. Here, as a bus with an internal combustion engine that could comfortably carry 24 passengers. Quite possibly the LMS would expect rather more to make the operating requirements of a speciaised vehicle viable. The unit did achieve some fifteen minutes advantage of steam working but the LMS did not show a lot of enthusiasm and a claim that it did not discharge fog detonators was almost seized upon by the company. They did show more interest in the Road-rail bus that ran between Byfield and the Welcombe Hotel at Stratford-upon-Avon but even this was not a great success.

L&GRP

One of the Churchward 2-6-0 '4300' class introduced 1911, this no 6336 is on the GWR lines north of Oxford on May 1, 1956. The LNWR signalbox on the right was demolished not long after this time. To the left the distant water tower seen over a fraction view of the bridge.

H C Casserley

Stanier 8F no 48655 makes a fine display in the chill of December 28, 1965 with a northbound freight at Oxford. This was just preceding the Oxford North Junction signalbox that controlled access onto the Oxford - Bletchley line through the World War II double track junction.

K C H Fairey

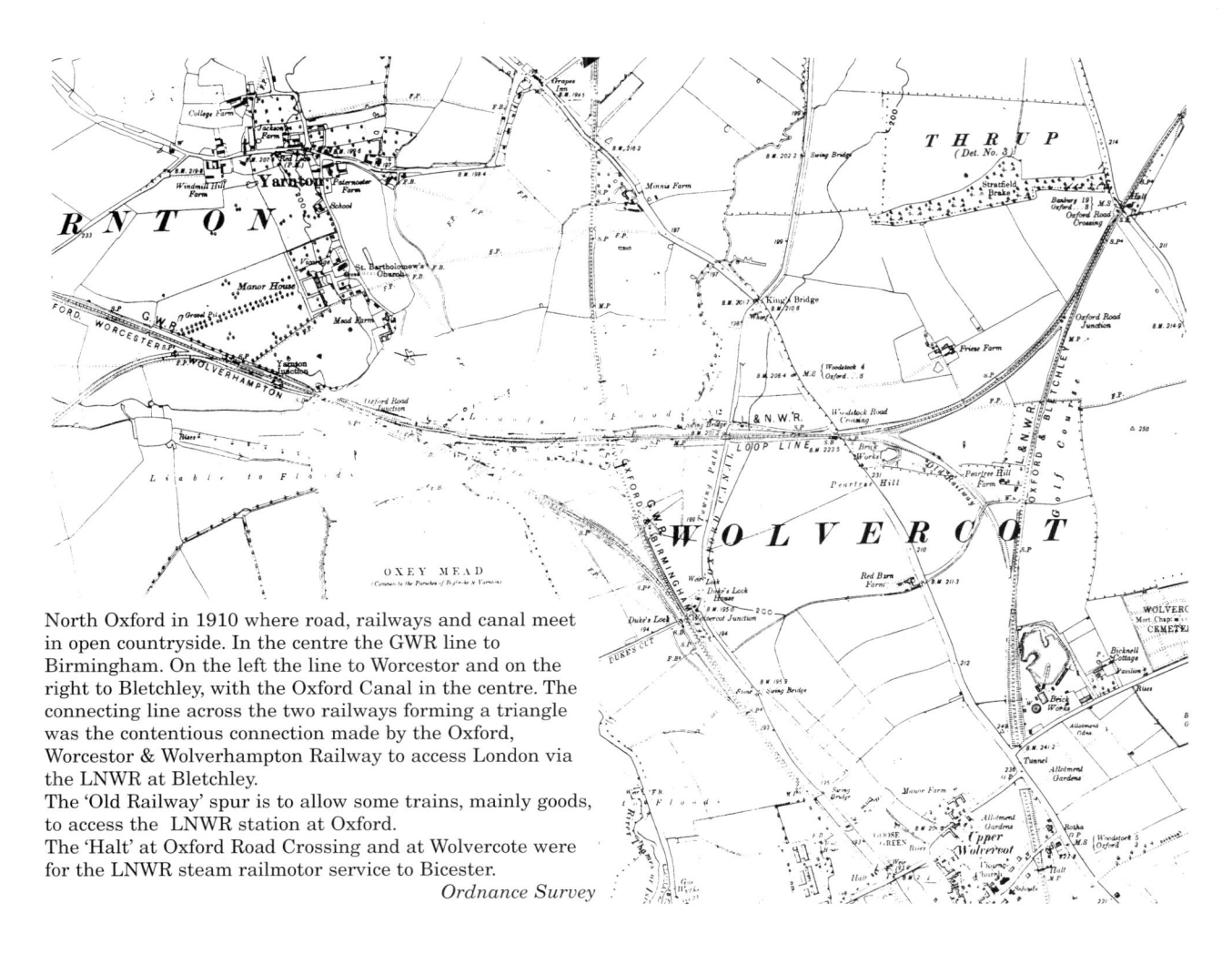

North Oxford in 1910 where road, railways and canal meet in open countryside. In the centre the GWR line to Birmingham. On the left the line to Worcestor and on the right to Bletchley, with the Oxford Canal in the centre. The connecting line across the two railways forming a triangle was the contentious connection made by the Oxford, Worcestor & Wolverhampton Railway to access London via the LNWR at Bletchley.

The 'Old Railway' spur is to allow some trains, mainly goods, to access the LNWR station at Oxford.

The 'Halt' at Oxford Road Crossing and at Wolvercote were for the LNWR steam railmotor service to Bicester.

Ordnance Survey

Once a proud representative of the LNWR now living out its final few years showing post World War Two grime and gloom, the 'Prince of Wales' class no 25845. Its fall from grace is all the more remarkable from a time when it was built as an extra locomotive of the class by Beardmore & Co in February 1924. It then carried a nameplate removed from no 819 of the class - 'Prince of Wales'. It was exhibited at Wembley at the British Empire Exhibition of the same year. It is seen here on March 15, 1946; it was withdrawn in November 1947.

H C Casserley

The Oxford North Junction was created out of an issue of railway politics when a company called the Oxford, Worcester & Wolverhampton Railway decided to leave GWR support and look to the LNWR for a connection to London, via Bletchley, rather than Oxford. A link was built across north Oxfordshire to connect the two railways, thus the junction. The siding alongside the train is in fact the connecting line curving away just beyond the last coach of the train. The LNWR built a signalbox here which was replaced in the mid-fifties with this new box which survived for about fifteen years. The fact that the signalman would hold OW&W trains in favour of the LNWR did not encourage the relationship. Eventually the OW&W was returned to the GWR under its absorbing the company- The West Midland Railway. The train is hauled by one of the British Railways Standard tanks with eight vehicles behind the bunker, which is an impressive length for the cross-country line at this time.

J D Edward

A valuable photograph historically of the road crossing at Oxford Road in the early 1930s, before the road bridge was built in 1936. A G2 class 0-8-0 takes a train of empty hopper wagons from South Wales back to Richard Thomas and Baldwins quarries in Northamptonshire, one quarry was near Blisworth.

K Pinder

The same location in 1980 from track position, the print above view is now blocked by the bridge. The signalbox was located close to the white box on the left. A siding was installed for a stone terminal. The bridge built in 1936 is alongside the site of original road and crossing that was on this side.

Bill Simpson

Standard class 4 4-6-0 arriving from Bletchley passing the Oxford Road stone terminal and sidings connecting with the Second World War grain silo, these were off to the right. The area where the sheep peacefully graze is now covered with the A34 connecting south traffic with the M40 near Bicester.

J D Edwards

Islip station looking towards Bicester on November 12, 1956. This station building would have dated from after January 25, 1881 when the original station was destroyed in a blizzard. This is not quite as alarming as it sounds as early country stations tended to be no more than cheaply built timber shelters with a platform little above rail level, most of the costs being expended on the nearby Stationmaster's house. The crossover would be for trains to access the single road siding on the 'down' side.
R M Casserley

Islip

The small village station at Islip was a remarkable feature of the branch being almost entirely built of timber. The Statiomaster's house close by was built in brick.

Islip is in effect the beginning of the line's crossing of the ancient tract of land called Otmoor. This is a level marshy ground that continues almost to Bicester.

The area of Otmoor is associated with civil unrest, with riots against enclosures in 1830. There have been tales of supernatural happenings, a ghostly Roman army crossing the marsh. Perhaps it was the marsh wizard that invoked the blizzard of January 25, 1881 when the station buildings were totally destroyed.

The role of the country station was fulfilled at Islip, with all the supply and cartage to fulfil the needs to the comparitive isolation in the nineteenth century. Coal deliveries, regular cattle wagons and horse boxes with considerable amounts of milk. The movement of milk from rural parts to London was an important part of the railways' responsibilities. It was also gathered for local milk processing manufactuory like the works at Buckingham of Thew, Hooker and Gilby.

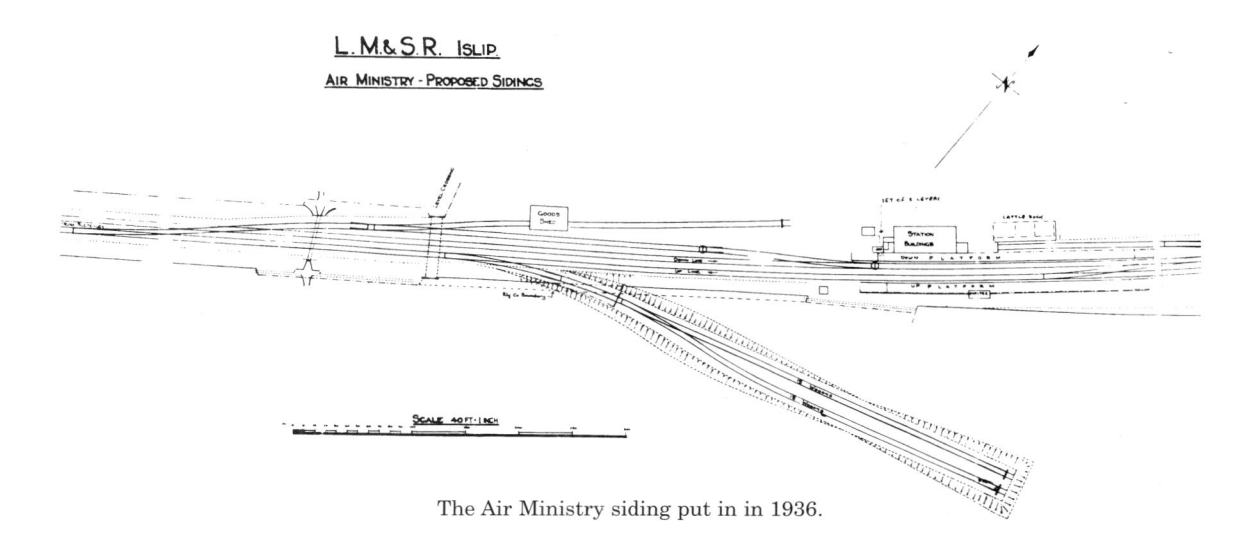

The Air Ministry siding put in in 1936.

The crossing shortly before Islip station on the five mile point from Oxford is over a lane that is a loop road from Islip to access a nearby farm. On the left is the crossing keeper's house whilst on the right is a hut that held the frame for the 'up' distant signal that was 'slotted' with the 'home' at Islip station. The 'down' distants that were 'slotted' with the station starter situated at the platform. The crossing was not a block post.

Bill Simpson Collection

A class 8F no 48359 on the 8.45 am ex Swanbourne pick-up goods passing west of Islip on September 28, 1963.

Peter E Baughan

Approaching Islip from Bicester on July 23, 1951 from behind engine no 40743 which was a Midland Railway design 4-4-0 2P. Just before the station the points lead off to the right to the MoD oil siding.

H C Casserley

There was also a daily tariff van that carried local produce in passenger trains with less urgent consignments being picked up by the daily pick-up goods train.

It was remarkable that during the late 1950s crossing keepers' houses along the line at Islip, Oddington, Langford Lane and Launton did not have a supply of fresh drinking water as this had to be brought in milk churns on the trains.

The station yard had a loop siding and a single end stop siding with a goods shed.

Two private sidings went into an original wartime Air Ministry fuel depot unlocked by Anette's key opened in 1941.

Although the station closed in 1968 it was reopened following the reinstatement of the passenger service from Oxford to Bicester in 1987.

From the same train at the station, note the brick built station house visible on the right.

H C Casserley

31

Looking towards Oxford in 1956.

Lens of Sutton

In 1959 a new Craven diesel multiple unit calls at Islip with a train for Bletchley.

Chris Hone

Bicester station in Oxfordshire limestone in a style adopted by the Buckinghamshire Railway at its principal stations. Bicester is on the 16 milepost. Note the 'Hawkseye' style nameboard of the LMS that has been suffixed with the name 'London Road' to distinguish it from the former GWR station in the town which became Bicester 'North'.

Bicester

The market town of Bicester was the largest centre of population between Bletchley and Oxford and this line was its only rail communication for sixty years until the arrival of the GWR in the town from Princes Risborough in 1910. This new line crossed the Bletchley - Oxford on the 19 mp.

The station at Bicester was attractively built in stone which prevails throughout the town. The Stationmaster's house close by was in a design matching with the station. Even the tiny weighbridge hut was also done to the same style.

In the latter days of the line the station building fell derelict and was finally demolished in 2000 to allow greater space for a coach company.

Close to Bicester was built a long siding entering the RAF aerodrome in 1927. This was probably for coal and it appears that wagons were horse drawn on the line which was built using concrete sleepers and was about half a mile long.

On the opposite side of the level crossing the line passes alongside a beautiful public park called Garth Park on the Bletchley side. The hunting box with its attractive flourishes of turrets and ornamental gables would have been visible from the train in years gone by.

The Bicester Gas Company that was close to the station on the 'up' side must have found their need for coal sufficiently fulfilled by bringing it by road from the station yard as no siding was ever built into the works. Later in the 1960s a naptha plant was built further along the line and this did have a siding and diesel locomotive.

The re-introduction of the railway service between Oxford and Bicester on Saturday May 9, 1987 was greeted enthusiastically. Unfortunately the Bicester Town station never had the advantage of car parking space of Bicester North, much of the land being turned over to garaging coaches. As a consequence the station has not enjoyed the success that might have followed had the parking availability been linked to that of the nearby Bicester Village shopping facility, which is enjoying something of an international reputation.

The Steam Railmotor, an attempt by the LNWR to provide a more economical passenger unit to fulfil a suburban role calling at six timber halts between Oxford and Bicester at Port Meadow, Wolvercote, Oxford Road, Oddington, Charlton and Wendlebury. The service began on October 20, 1905. There were seven journeys each way costing 1 shilling (5p) for the entire journey. Standing in a dark winter evening on one of the lonely Otmoor platforms with a few faint oil lamps for lighting sounds a bit testy! The engine to the vehicle was enclosed in the far end on the photograph but of course it was fitted with controls to be driven from both ends. Note the folding steps and the low Bicester station platform. The service was withdrawn with the outbreak of World War 1. It was not an unqualified success with regular break downs and was hated by the footplate crew being so enclosed. Much more successful was the steam locomotive push-pull method that superseded it.

Real Photographs

A new signalbox was built in 1942 to control the entrance to the then new Bicester Military Railway. It was described as an LMS ARP box which presented a very austere but robust design. It became 'Bicester No 2' and was demolished out of service replaced by a ground frame in 1973.

Bill Simpson

A dmu entering Bicester from the Bletchley in the early 1960's. The signalbox was a type 4 LNWR and probably replaced an early Saxby box. The scene is now much changed with only the distant row of houses remaining with a single line of railway.

Richard Keeys

This view, looking towards the station, was taken in 1980 showing the entrance to the goods yard and ground frame used to control it.

Bill Simpson

Military railways found the outstanding loco to serve their purposes was the Hunslet 'Austerity' 0-6-0 saddletank. Bicester took a complement of forty-five passing through their system along with numerous other steam types. Here is no 197 *Sapper* that was changed to *Northiam*, works no 3797/93 at Graven Hill on August 16, 1965. This was the last steam locomotive to work on the system and is now preserved on the Kent & East Sussex Railway.

Ted Evans

The saddletanks were vacuum fitted to operate the considerable passenger trains on the military railway during the war so they were also able to haul the occasional enthusiasts' special afterwards as seen here with the a Locomotive Club of Great Britain train in the 1960's.

Peter Waylett

One of the Andrew Barcay diesel hydraulic engines that replaced the steam fleet. These handsome 0-8-0 engines were strong but very heavy for the system that was built with wartime expediency. *Royal Pioneer* no 624 arrived on BMR December 1965 and was sold for scrap in May 1985. From the 1980's these were replaced by 'Vanguard' and 'Steelman Royale' 0-4-0 engines by Hill and they are working there at the time of writing.

Bill Simpson

A view from the signal box with the station buildings just visible through the windows. The type 4 LNWR box was situated alongside the level crossing which was once opened and closed by turning a nautical style wheel.

Bill Simpson

The view in 1980 of a new siding that was installed in 1967 for a gas plant that was built on the land beyond the distant gates to extract town gas from naptha. The first train of naptha ran from Parkston Quay on February 19, 1968. The last ran on June 13, 1969. Apparently the process was not a success and the works was soon demolished.

Bill Simpson

From the same location in 2006. Industry at Bicester has expanded rapidly with ribbon development along all of its major roads. In this there has been no role for the railway as both stations are concentrated on passenger usage. Transport progression is drawn more into question as total reliance on one system proves vulnerable with fuel and environmental factors being of great public concern.

Bill Simpson

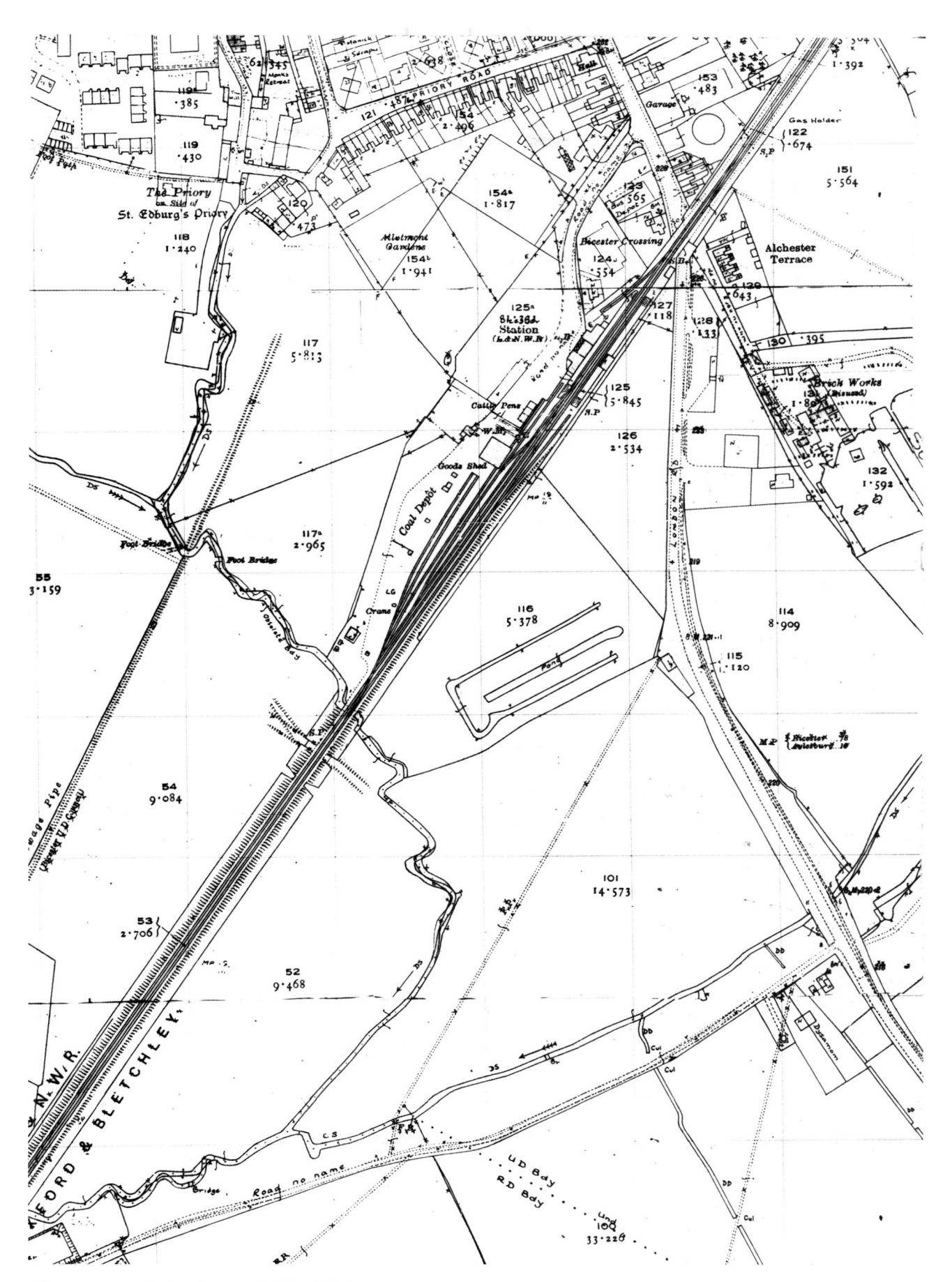

Bicester station during the period of the LNWR in its most complete form. Much building has taken place around the area over the years and the new modern shopping complex called 'Bicester Village' is situated in the open field space on the 'up' side near the entrance to the goods yard.

Ordnance Survey

Throughout the second World War a Royal Engineers' train ran between the camp and the station using a coach originally attributed to the Rother Valley Railway. It is seen here approaching the station in 1952 passing the huge timber goods shed. In the distance can be seen the Bicester No 2 signalbox controlling entrance to the camp.

John R Batts

Lament for a country station. A photograph of Bicester in 1980 when much of it was intact apart from the removal of the 'down' platform. The distant gas holder remains on the works the site, which is now covered with a housing development.

Bill Simpson

The station front in 1979 looking fairly derelict. It is not difficult to imagine that it would have been quite attractive at one time. The perfectly balanced gables enclosing the portico entrance. And alongside the now twisted line of LNWR 'unclimeable' fencing.

Bill Simpson

Bicester North after the runaway of Prairie 4105 on December 23, 1963. The engine "lost its feet' on an ironstone train and the crew, when they realised a hopeless situation, jumped clear as the engine careered on and toppled over the bridge into the Launton Road. On being retrieved it was placed in the yard in front of the station where it was cut up after being condemned in February 1964. This area is now the station car park.

An 0-4-0 diesel mechanical locomotive was employed to work the gas siding, seen here in October 1969. Details were No JF4210136/58.

Ted Evans

Immediately eyecatching and picturesque; the little station at the level crossing for the road between Launton, Stratton Audley and Marsh Gibbon. The single siding is out of view on the right.

H C Casserley

Launton

Not far east of Bicester was another small village station for Launton situated on the road crossing from Launton to Stratton Audley. It is only a matter of about a mile from the village to the station and as it is about two miles from the village to Bicester station by road this rather suggests that some passengers would hold the choice of station in the balance; especially as all trains stopped at Bicester and only a select few stopped at Launton. Also the introduction of the steam railmotor service from Bicester to Oxford from October 20, 1905 would be another factor. Consequently the station could not have hoped to have considerable passenger receipts. In 1853 the station had five trains calling each way and by 1909 the same number. In 1921 this had increased to six trains each way. In 1942 this was reduced to four trains 'up' from Oxford and three 'down', with surprisingly two trains each way on Sunday, when there had never been more than one before. This became even more remarkable in 1953 when it became seven and six, which continued until closure in 1967.

For coal deliveries and milk collection that would be another matter as the area has been, and still is, intensively agricultural. Milk collection was largely the reason for running a Sunday train. The Goslings of Stratton Audley, a centre for fine bloodstock, brought their horses to the station for transporting.

The original station platform was edged with the blocks first used on the permanent way of the London & Birmingham Railway. The station house was built abutting into the embankment of the line at this point with the crossing keeper's house on the other side of the line. Crossing Keepers being required to be attentive for 24 hours each day. In 1921 a mineral train ran from Nuneaton off Bletchley at 2.00 am arriving at Oxford at 4.15 am, meaning that it would probably pass over Launton level crossing about 3.30 am.

It may seem romantic now, but the station house did not have any electricity supply and illumination was with oil lamps.

Apart from the Crossing Keeper's house and some of the platform all has been demolished. It is now an open crossing.

A view towards Marsh Gibbon in the 1950's.

Wolverton Living Archive / Arthur Grigg

Looking towards Bicester with an ex Midland 4F entering with a passnger train in the 1950s The timber cover in the foreground conceals the signalling cables, leading to the frame on the right,

Wolverton Living Archive / Arthur Grigg

The view from the train allows a better view of the actual size of the station building that was deceptively built alongside the embankment, in fact being two stories with top rooms adjacent to the platform.

H C Casserley

Looking towards Bicester in the early 1980s when the station was derelict and the crossing was an automatic half barrier crossing. These were removed and it is now without gates and controlled only on the warning lights.

Bill Simpson

The station derelict in the early 1980s. All trace of this has now gone and only the restored crossing house remains as a private residence.

Bill Simpson

OXFORD & BLETCHLEY BRANCH.
1st, 2nd, and 3rd Class by all Trains.

From Oxford.	WEEK DAYS.						SUNDAYS	To Oxford.	WEEK DAYS.						SUNDAYS
	morn	morn	morn	noon	aft.	aft.	morn		morn	morn	morn	aft.	aft.	aft.	morn
Oxford	7 50	...	10 0	12 0	2 30	4 35	7 30	9 15	London—Euston	7 15	9 0	11 0	3 0	5 15	7 0	10 0
Islip	8 0	...	10 11	...	2 40	4 45	7 40	9 26	Bletchley	8 30	10 15	12 20	4 30	6 35	9 10	11 35
Bicester	8 12	...	10 24	12 19	2 53	4 58	7 54	9 41	Swanbourne	8 41	...	...	4 41	6 46	...	...
Launton	8 19	...	...	...	...	...	8 2	...	Winslow	8 47	10 32	12 38	4 46	6 52	9 26	11 51
Claydon	8 33	...	10 39	...	3 9	5 15	8 16	9 59	Verney Junction	8 55	10 43	12 46	4 53	7 0	...	...
Verney Junction	8 40	...	10 45	12 37	3 13	5 22	...	...	Claydon	8 59	10 48	12 52	5 0	7 5	9 40	12 3
Winslow	8 46	...	10 52	12 42	3 20	5 28	8 24	10 11	Launton	9 10	...	...	...	...	...	...
Swanbourne	9 1	...	11 0	...	3 26	5 38	8 34	10 21	Bicester	9 15	11 4	1 10	5 21	7 23	9 58	12 19
Bletchley	9 15	...	11 12	1 0	3 40	5 50	8 45	10 35	Islip	9 27	11 16	1 23	5 35	7 35	10 10	12 33
London—Euston	10 35	...	12 30	2 30	5 30	7 10	10 5	1 50	Oxford	9 40	11 30	1 35	5 50	7 50	10 25	12 45

BANBURY & BUCKINGHAM BRANCH.
1st, 2nd, and 3rd Class by all Trains.

From Banbury.	WEEK DAYS.					SUNDAYS		To Banbury.	WEEK DAYS.						SUNDAYS	
	morn	morn	aft.	aft.	aft.	morn	aft.		morn	morn	morn	aft.	aft.	aft.	morn	morn
Banbury	7 55	9 50	2 10	4 25	7 15	...	4 15	London—Euston	7 15	9 0	11 0	3 0	5 15	7 0	...	10 0
Farthinghoe	8 2	9 59	2 18	4 33	7 23	...	4 26	Bletchley	8 30	10 15	12 20	4 30	6 30	9 10	5 45	11 40
Brackley	8 14	10 10	2 30	4 45	7 40	...	4 41	Swanbourne	8 41	...	...	4 36	6 41	...	...	11 51
Buckingham	8 29	10 28	2 46	5 1	7 57	6 40	4 57	Winslow	8 47	10 32	12 38	4 41	6 46	9 26	6 0	11 57
Verney Junction	8 43	10 41	2 55	5 15	8 11	6 52	5 11	Verney Junction	8 57	10 50	12 48	4 48	6 52	...	6 20	...
Winslow	8 51	10 46	3 5	5 20	8 17	7 0	5 17	Buckingham	9 11	11 10	1 2	5 1	7 5	9 49	6 32	12 16
Swanbourne	9 1	11 0	3 14	5 39	8 34	7 8	5 25	Brackley	9 26	11 35	1 19	5 18	7 19	10 2	...	12 33
Bletchley	9 15	11 12	3 25	5 43	8 45	7 20	5 37	Farthinghoe	9 38	...	1 31	5 30	7 34	...	...	12 50
London—Euston	10 35	12 30	4 40	7 10	10 5	8 35	8 10	Banbury	9 45	...	1 40	5 38	7 42	10 25	...	1 0

BEDFORD & HITCHIN BRANCH.
1st and 3rd Class by all trains. No trains on Sundays.

To Hitchin.	morn	morn	aft.	aft.	aft.
Bedford	7 50	12 28	4 50	7 20	...
Cardington	7 59	12 38	5 0	7 29	...
Southill	8 9	12 47	5 15	7 45	...
Shefford	8 16	12 53	5 15	7 45	...
Henlow	8 21	1 0	5 22	7 55	...
Hitchin	8 37	1 8	5 30	8 3	...
London—King's†	9 45	3 25	6 38	9 15	...

From Hitchin.	morn	morn	aft.	aft.
London—King's†	5 15	9 0	1 10	5 5
Hitchin	6 20	10 0	2 55	6 5
Henlow	6 27	10 8	3 4	6 14
Shefford	6 33	10 14	3 10	6 21
Southill	6 39	10 20	3 19	6 27
Cardington	6 49	10 27	3 30	6 30
Bedford	6 55	10 35	3 40	6 45

Newport & Wolverton.

From Newport	mrn	mrn	mrn	morn	morn	aft.	aft.	aft.	aft.
Newport	5 30	7 45	9 20	10 50	12	5 2	4 0	5 4	6 10
Bradwell	...	7 55	9 30	11 0	12 15	2 48	4 15	5	6 20
Wolverton	5 41	8 0	9 32	11 2	12 17	2 55	4 17	5	6 25

From Wolverton	mrn	mrn	mrn	morn	morn	aft.	aft.	aft.	aft.
Wolverton	8 30	9 45	11 35	12 55	3 25	4 30	5 40	6 48	9 10
Bradwell	8 32	9 47	11 38	12 57	3 27	4 32	5 42	6 50	9 12
Newport	8 42	9 57	11 50	12 47	3 37	4 42	5 52	7 0	9 22

A timetable of 1883 showing Launton not very well served whilst all other stations had every train calling. Of particular interest is the way that some 'up' and 'down' trains are joined and separated at Winslow still, even though Verney Junction station now exists and would have siding accommodation. This would endorse Winslow's importance as a township on the line.

Author's Collection

Marsh Gibbon station seen in a backward glance from a Bletchley bound train on July 12, 1955. The signalling frame and instruments were held in the section of the building with the bay windows.

R M Casserley

Marsh Gibbon

The village of Marsh Gibbon only acquired its station on August 2, 1880. Presumably the villagers had to use Launton station until then. No doubt the burgeoning demand for coal inwards and milk outwards had something to do with it. It had become knowledge in the city that Sir Edward Watkin had plans for the district which took the form of the arrival of the Metropolitan Railway at Verney Junction less than six miles away by 1891.

When they did receive their station however it proved to be a commodious arrangement with robust timber buildings of modular construction produced on standard patterns at Crewe. The station house was also of an LNWR standard building pattern at the foot of the driveway leading up to the embanked station.

The station closed on the last day of 1967.

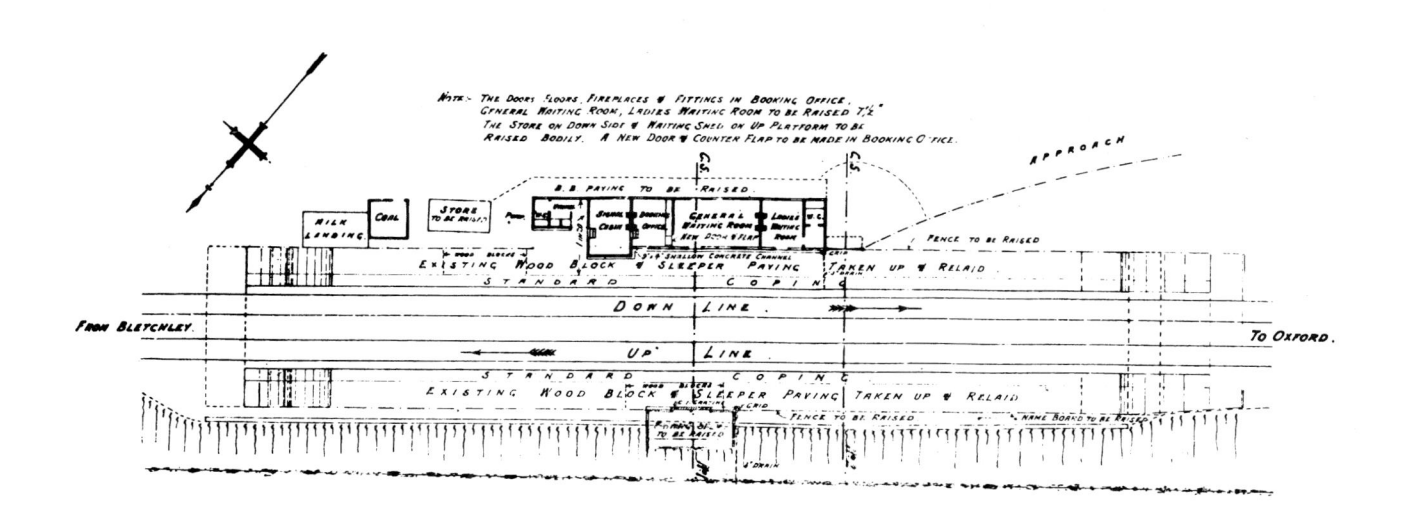

A fine grouping of railway childen in 1904 in probable Sunday best. The Stationmaster finely attired with high starched collar and frock coat with gleaming buttons. The porter more basically attired representing the hard physical labour demanded by a lot of handling that would be required even at this rural station.

Leicestershire & Rutland Public Records Office

Marsh Gibbon station as it would have appeared under the LNWR with woodwork in buff and stone and lower quadrant signals. Of note is the siding to the cattle dock on the far 'down' side that has gates across the tracks, probably to ensure that no beasts are able to make their escape that way

L&GRP

Approach to the station on the raised driveway from the Marsh Gibbon to Stratton Audley Road. Mr H C Casserley often used his car to provide an extra interest in his photographs of stations as here.

H C Casserley

Looking towards Claydon, Marsh Gibbon & Poundon station on September 28, 1963. Painted now in the cream and dark red of the British Railways colours. Note the lower quadrant semaphores have been replaced with standard BR tubular post upper quadrant signals.

Peter Baughan

A Stanier 2-8-0 8 Freight no 48440 heading towards Oxford through Claydon station on Friday, September 7, 1962 at 3.05 pm. Note the LNWR employees houses adjoining the goods yard behind the station

Andrew Bratton

Claydon

Claydon was a collective name for all the surrounding Claydons, prominent of course being Claydon House, home of one of the promoters for the building of the railway - Sir Harry Verney.

This station carried greater architectural presentation with its decorative barge boarding and station canopy, the only one on the line apart from Oxford. The platform was of similar construction as the one at Launton. The station house was part of the station buildings and was of considerable size. Alongside the goods yard are some houses built to the pattern of the LNWR for station staff; these are now in private hands

The platform buildings survived for quite some time after the line closed to passengers. The station house was demolished much earlier than the station buildings. These were removed some time in the late 1980s.

Between Marsh Gibbon and Claydon was also the connection with the Great Central Railway and a siding to what had originally been Itter's Brick Co Ltd. This eventually became part the brickworks of the London Brick Company. The Great Central Railway crossed over the line at the milepost 13. This line was a prominent casualty of the Beeching report of 1963. The passenger service at Calvert station was closed in March of that year. The entire line north of Claydon Junction was removed in 1969.

The last brick train left Calvert Brickworks on December 8, 1977. The connection between the Oxford - Bletchley ran alongside the GCR embankment for about a mile. This siding created some amusement to locals as it had been lightly laid across the ridge and furrow of a field so the train looked as if it was rolling over the ocean. The enlargement of a knothole in adjoining land gradually eroded the trackbed and with traffic receding the siding was abandoned. It was replaced by the wartime connection.

A time in the early 1960s with a 'Royal Scot' class 4-6-0 no 46122 *Royal Ulster Rifleman* passing over the former Great Central Railway bridge over the Oxford - Bletchley line near Calvert with Marylebone train.

Andrew Bratton

A class 4 Standard 4-6-0 no 75028 of Bletchley shed taking a parcels train to Oxford from Bletchley at 7.15 pm on Tuesday, May 19, 1964.

Andrew Bratton

On the other side of the bridge, evident in the distance, is the connection with the former Great Central line made during World War II. Although the connection remains in use to the present day, for the landfill trains, the signalbox has gone to preservation on the Swindon & Cricklade Railway, the only remaining portion of the erstwhile Midland & South Western Junction Railway. Modern signalling has now replaced the semaphores on this view on December 29, 1967.

K C H Fairey

In the 1930s a number of ex-Midland 4-4-0 types operated the passenger service. One is seen here approaching the Claydon area with the 5.54 pm Oxford to Cambridge train on May 13, 1939.

H C Casserley

One of the former 7F 0-8-0 freight engines known as a G2 no 9434 shunting Itter's brickworks siding at Calvert on May 13, 1939. The type 5 LNWR signalbox is partially visible whilst the train is held on the line awaiting the completion of the shunting manoeuvre.

H C Casserley

A view along the former Great Central line at Calvert with a Jubilee class no 45598 *Basutoland* heading north on a Cup Final special from Wembley Stadium at 6.35 pm on May 25, 1963.
Andrew Bratton

The wartime curve built at Claydon from the former GCR main line to the Oxford - Bletchley photographed from a dmu in 1981.
Bill Simpson

Claydon as it looked in 1980, the 'up' side platform had long been removed and the station house demolished. The station buidings were spared for a further ten years, possibly they were used by pw gangs for shelter.

Bill Simpson

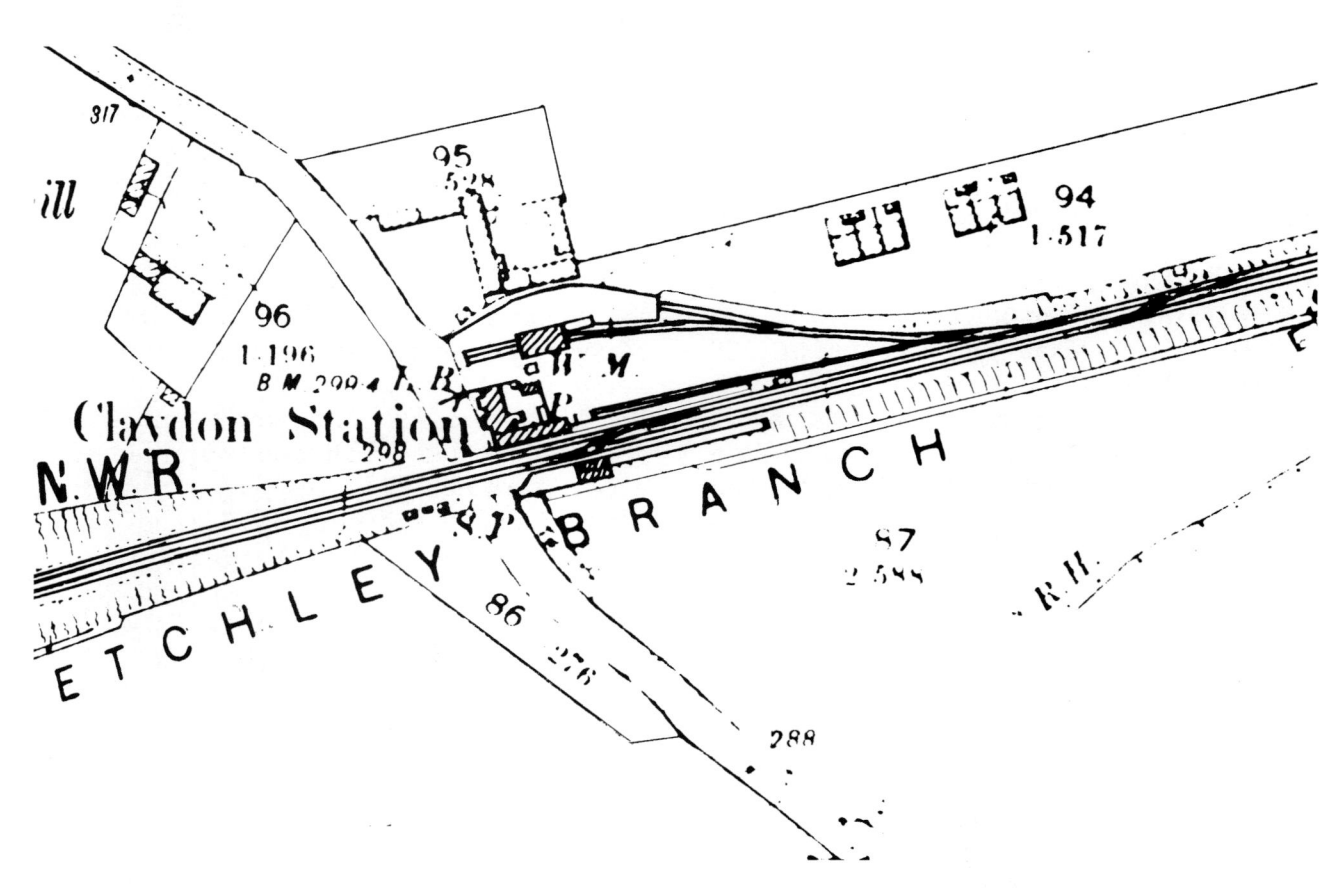

Claydon station in 1886, the group of houses adjoining the goods yard were built by the LNWR for their employees and remain still.

Ordnance Survey

The signalman leans out of his box at Verney Junction to receive a single line electric train staff from the driver of a class 4 Standard 4-6-0 75038 that has probably just come off the Banbury branch with a pick-up freight on Wednesady, August 29. 1962.
Andrew Bratton

Verney Junction

A station named after Sir Harry Verney that came to be the nodel point of the north Bucks lines. The line to Banbury was the first to open in May 1850, it was hoped that this would be a main line, but it was not to be.

The line to Oxford progressed at the same time opening there in 1851.

A line from Aylesbury arrived here in 1868 called the Aylesbury & Buckingham Railway. This line had a very parlous existence until it was rescued in 1891 when the Metropolitan Railway in its progress north from London absorbed it as part of its system. Thus this country junction acquired a status that endeared it in railway history with its cluster of houses and a hotel that is still in use as a restaurant.

On that subject of dining; in Metropolitan days the station enjoyed the delightful view of gleaming Pullman cars awaiting passengers to take them right into the heart of the city over the Circle line. The journey would be reversed later in the day and the cars would be kept at Aylesbury.

At the rear of the Verney Arms were places to store carriages with stables for the horses.

Things began to wither in the 1930s with the end of the passenger service to Aylesbury in 1936.

The Metropolitan was taken over by London Transport in 1933. London Transport envisaged continuing the Metropolitan line services, pending electrification, no further north than Amersham.

They recinded the service north of Aylesbury to the LNER who continued with goods workings only to Verney Junction. These probably continued until World War II when the connection between the ex-GCR and the LMS at Claydon was built. This continues to be used to the present day.

The defunct section to Verney was used for old wagon and coach storage.

The line to Buckingham and Banbury was totally closed some thirty years later in 1966.

Verney Junction continued bravely with its attractive gardens delighting travellers to the very end. It is still an attractive hamlet but with the railway so reduced it challenges the imagination to think of it how it once was.

A view looking towards Bletchley on June 18, 1955. The Metropolitan signalbox is visible beyond the bridge.
H C Casserley

Looking down from the footbridge on June 18, 1955 the lines of the Metropolitan have not yet been lifted. The very rural nature of the junction station can be well appreciated in this view. All that remains now is the footpath crossing.
H C Casserley

A little east of Verney Junction an Oxford bound goods train hauled by a more unusual visitor to the line an LNER J69 0-6-0 no 64803. The date is June 18, 1955. The overgrown tracks on the right are those of the former Metropolitan Railway.

H C Casserley

Looking east towards Oxford on March 18, 1955.

H C Casserley

In the days of long six wheel trains on the Oxford - Bletchley line a 'Problem' class no 1429 'Alfred Paget' with an Oxford train. The vehicles close to the engine are horse boxes.
LNWR Society

Looking very wintery and bleak with the removal of the Met lines in the foreground. Only the remotely isolated garden stork watches class D5XX hauling a goods as it rumbles through in progress towards Bletchley at 12.00 pm on Saturday, January 15, 1966..

Andrew Bratton

The Banbury branch pick-up freight passing through Verney Junction towards Bletchley

Andrew Bratton

No view of the station should pass without reference to the well known elaboration of its garden design. It was a tradition that the staff at Verney responded to in competitions with more than average enthusiasm. The building behind was the booking office with the footbridge steps immediately in the rear.

H C Casserley

On September 22, 1962 The South Bedfordshire Locomotive Club ran a rail tour called 'The Banburian', touring the Oxford and Banbury lines hauled by one of the ex-LNWR 7F 0-8-0s. The old Met sidings found use as coach storage.

Andrew Bratton

An ex-LNWR 7F 0-8-0 hauling a loose coupled freight through Winslow at midday in the summer of 1960.

Andrew Bratton

Winslow

Winslow is a town similar in size to Bicester and had a station situated on milepost 7. When the line was opened trains for both Banbury and Oxford were split at Winslow because Bletchley had no capacity to operate properly as a junction. They arrived from Bletchley as one train to Winslow being sent from there independently and rejoined on return. Consequently Winslow had a turntable and water tank house for the engines and long sidings to store coaches for local services. This prevailed until Bletchley developed as a much more commodious junction with extended capacity. The practice seems to have continued in reduced form right up until the 1900s even with the development of Verney Junction

The station area at Winslow now has been transformed enormously with new houses being built there. The station building was in a very derelict state when it was finally demolished in the early 1990's.

With future rail hopes of a Milton Keynes - Aylesbury service Winslow could have a new role to play serving the expansion of its community with a new station on a new site in the same area.

Looking back from a 'down' train at the Winslow 'up' platform on June 1, 1956.

R M Casserley

The style of the Buckinghamshire Railway is evident in the similarity of Winslow to Bicester.

H C Casserley

A remarkable visitor on the line, a 'Britannia' class 4-6-2 pacific no 70019 *Lightning* of Cardiff shed on Saturday, June 8, 1963. It is hauling a short train of parcels/perishables vans from Crewe to Marylebone. It will pass over the Claydon connection to join the ex-GCR line.

Andrew Bratton

'The Banburian' called at Winslow to take water. Note the window ledge close to the platform surface. This was due to the platform height being raised for modern coach stock from 1880s onwards.

Andrew Bratton

The railcar experiment of 1956 saw the first dmu type stock on the line. In the 1960's the chevron 'cats whisker' front design was replaced with the higher visibility yellow panel. Here no M79901 is on the 2.58 pm to Bletchley from Buckingham on Saturday, September 22, 1962.

Andrew Bratton

Super streamlined diesel power in the form of the dmu Pullman that operated on the Western Region from Paddington to Birmingham over the GWR/GCR Joint line. It is passing through Winslow on its way to Wembley Stadium for the FA Cup Final on May 2, 1964. It was not a popular design, with a reputation for rough riding at high speed.

Andrew Bratton

The class 4 Standard 4-6-0's obviously operated much of the freight work in the final years of the line. Here no 75020 is working through Winslow to Bletchley at 10.00 am on Saturday, July 13, 1963.

Andrew Bratton

The sidings at Winslow holding passenger stock on May 18, 1959. This may well be a storage routine continuing from the days of Winslow's important role in storing and reassembling stock in the days when trains were separated and joined there for Banbury and Oxford.

F A Blencowe

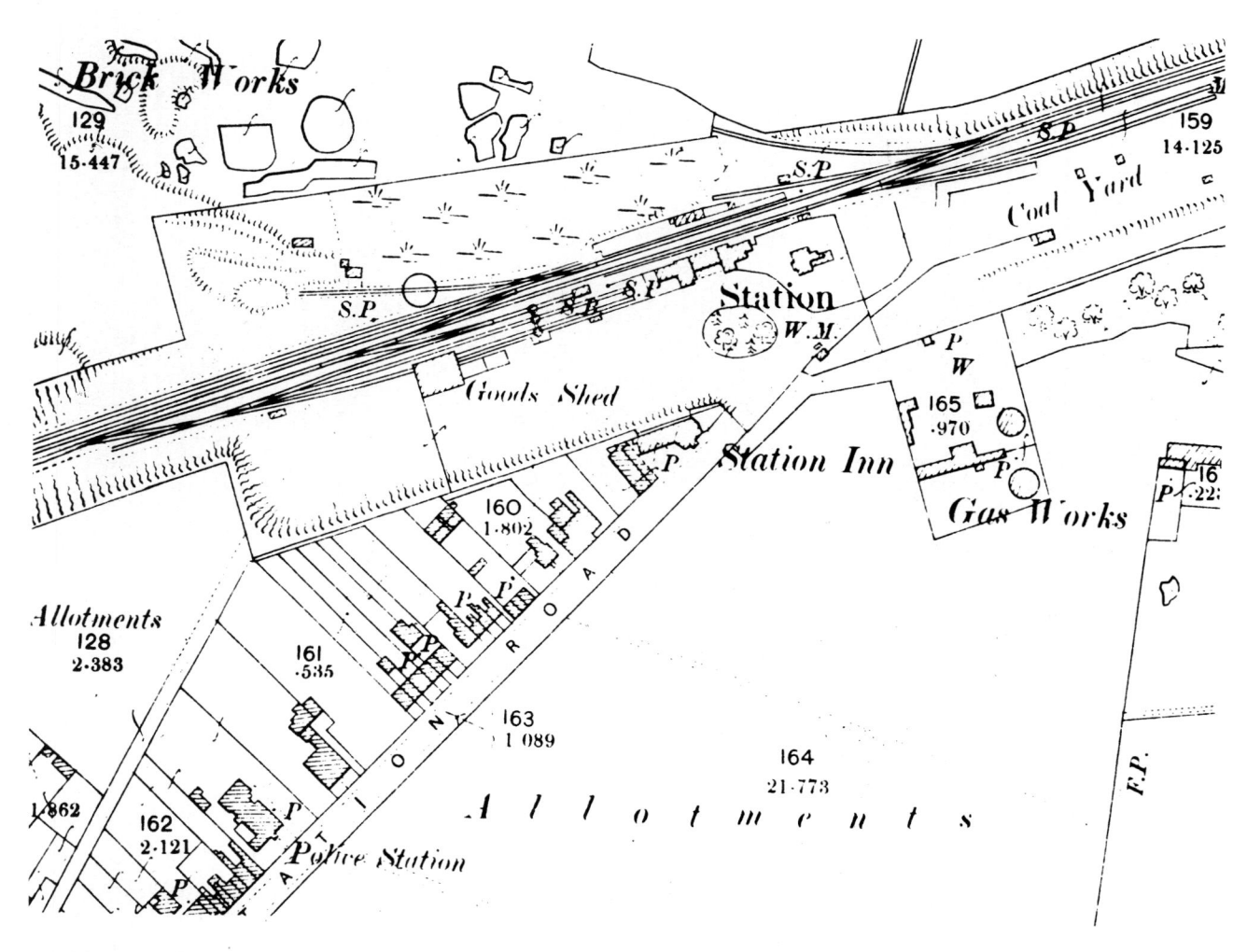

Winslow must have been a very interesting place in 1850 when the line opened. All the evidence is clear on this map. As trains would be joined and separated for the two destinations this would cause a number of light engine movements, thus the turntable. On the Oxford branch five passenger trains were formed with coaches for Banbury in the rear. These were detatched at Winslow and worked forward by the branch engine. Return working was by the same means the Banbury vehicles being attached to the front of the Oxford portion. Although the lines between Winslow and Verney Junction were converted to double track on December 1, 1875 the LNWR continued to work the trains in the same way until the 1900s. Acrimoniously the LNWR preferred to forget about the existance of Verney Junction station until the arrival of the Metropolitan in 1894. This brought the rebuilding of that station and reappraisal by the LNWR. Curiously, 'down' trains divided there, but the 'up' trains were still joined at Winslow. The sidings shown here as the coal yard were also used for storing coaching stock. The two sidings on the 'up' side probably held trains in waiting as a portion would be brought from one of the other destinations. The station front was superbly done with a circular green and large tree. Since the demolition of the station buildings this as been built over with houses. Doubtless the Station Inn would have been busily engaged in sustaining many waiting travellers.

Ordnance Survey

On April 19, 1959 the Buckingham - Bletchley 10.00 am train at Swanbourne which would have connected with the single unit railcar at Buckingham. The engine is one of the Ivatt 2-6-2 tanks which brought a certain briskness to branch line, working after ageing antedeluvian LNWR types.

R M Casserley

Swanbourne

Swanbourne station could not be better suited to its name, it is located a mile or so from the village. It exemplifys the character of rural Buckinghamshire with a station of chalet style gables that have remarkably survived from 1850. It speaks so clearly now of another age, with high speed Pendolino electrics hurtling by a few miles away on the main line. There are now probably very few village stations of that age so intact and it deserves to remain so. It is however unlikely be revived on the introduction of any new service but would provide an interesting diversion for passengers on such trains passing through or possibly as a request stop.

Between Winslow and Swanbourne was the eleven road marshalling yard built during the World War 2. This was a wartime necessity that when it became no longer essential melded into decline and neglect. To return the countryside to its previous tranquillity

In 1950 it was realised with some alarm locally that this yard was to be developed to become a large new marshalling yard amongst a group of nationwide yards in an automised freight movement orbital system around London. Part of this was the new flyover at Bletchley that was in fact built. The Beeching plan effectively nullified the practice of the marshalling yard system and as a consequnce this part of the plan was never fulfilled.

The countryside around Swanbourne is more than a visual delight. It represents the kind of green acres that we need for our peace of mind. So the notorious reputation of the doctor as the grim reaper of railways is not entirely fair, although the salvation of Swanbourne was not his intention.

Between Swanbourne and Bletchley industry did not impose as it had in many large industrial towns. Brick making at the Newton Longville brick plant of the London Brick Company came in the 1900's and developed into a more capacious plant. This was connected with a steeply graded siding which ceased to be used in 1964. The works continued producing with road distribution until the plant was closed in the 1980's and subsequently demolished.

Looking towards Oxford in 1933 with a view of the single siding on the 'down' side *L&GRP*

The small country station of Swanbourne. the design echoes that of the long ago demolished Farthinghoe on the Banbury branch.

Andrew Bratton

A view of the entire building from the Oxford side in 1981 when the line was still double track.

Bill Simpson

A view from the 1930s with LNWR nameboard and the lower quadrant platform starter.

The sidings of eleven roads near Swanbourne built during the second World War. This view in the late 1960s is of a Black Five at the Newton Longville end. Pick-up goods trains on the two branches tended to be shunted and rostered from here until it was removed in the early 1970s. This of course would have been the site of a huge new marshalling complex if the plans had been continued.

D Barrow

Bletchley station front in 1960. The ornate Flemish style gables and arcading is reminiscent of buildings on the Northampton & Peterborough Railway which are the work of J W Livock. It might therefore be reasonably concluded that this is his work also. The balance has been seriously disturbed by the dormer roof extension and its narrowness may not suit the modern 'wide mouth' approach but its demolition was a significant architectural loss.

Author's Collection

Bletchley

Bletchley acquired a station in 1840, two years after the opening of the London & Birmingham Railway on April 9, 1838 replacing a temporary station at Denbigh Hall. The first station was a very modest affair, looking a little like the layout of Launton. It is situated alongside the Buckingham to Fenny Stratford road which the railway crossed with a gated crossing. Both Buckingham and Fenny Stratford were established on the Grand Junction Canal, the latter with very busy wharves.

With the opening of the line to Bedford in 1846, and the the line to Banbury and Oxford in 1850 and 1851 respectively the station developed a great deal with a new station building and a hotel in the Jacobean style.

With the development of the main line the road crossing was soon dispensed with and a bridge over the road was built. Further, a new route was opened to Northampton and widening with extra lines came between 1875 and 1888 increasing Bletchley's work load as it entered the role of an important junction.

An early inadequate steam shed received storm damage so it was replaced by a large steam shed built to the design of F W Webb. A large coach shed was also built alongside the Oxford branch to house the stock for working the cross-country route and the suburban sets for working to London Euston.

In terms of industry a huge brickworks was opened and worked by the London brick Company alongside the main line.

Alterations and improvements were ongoing up until World War 1. Further renovation work was undertaken in 1953 with a £20,000 facelift, a new refreshment room and extensive electric lighting.

A concrete flyover was built above the junction connecting the cross-country route whilst avoiding the complications with the main line. This was opened in 1962. As already described, Dr Beeching had decreed that the marshalling yard system was an anachronism and that the new method of working goods trains should be as 'block' trains running point to point. Consequently the flyover was caught as an incomplete scheme emanating from a system now outmoded. It never realised anything like its benefits as a capital undertaking.

A reminder of the one time dependency of the Royal Mail as sacks are organised alongside rebuilt 'Patriot' class no 45530 'Sir Frank Ree' in 1964 on a parcels train on Saturday, June 8, 1963..

Andrew Bratton

Beneath the bulk of the new Oxbridge line flyover 4-6-2 Pacific *Britannia* swings across the 'down' fast line onto the Oxford branch on its way to Wembley Stadium with an FA Cup Final special on Saturday, May 2, 1964.

Andrew Bratton

74

One of the roaming workhorses, a Stanier 2-6-4 tank no 42431 in platform 4 after arriving with a workmens' train at 12.30 pm on Saturday, January 25, 1964.

Andrew Bratton

The large project to follow was the resignalling of the west coast main line. This took place at Bletchley district in June 1965. Most of the mechanical signalboxes were closed and all signalling control was electronic in the new panel box on the south 'down' side. This box formed a link between Rugby in the north and Watford in the south. Semaphores were of course replaced by multiple aspect signalling.

However the new works heralded the beginning of decline as a major operational centre.

The steam locomotive shed was closed in

Some of the lesser breeds of LNWR engines lasted until late in the period of the LMS, some still being used in the times of British Railways. The Webb 'Coal Tank' seen here was one such. On Bletchley shed they were used on the Newport Pagnell, Aylesbury and Dunstable branches. No 7763 seen here on September 11, 1937 lasted until March 1946 from being introduced in 1886.

H C Casserley

75

Bletchley on July 3, 1948 and rebuilt 'Jubilee' no 45735 'Comet' arrives with the 6.29 am Watford - Bletchley train. The building behind was the Bletchley Post Office.

H C Casserley

1965 and demolished shortly afterwards. The area is now the car park. It was replaced immediately with a new Bletchley District Electric Depot which also carried running repairs on electrics and diesels.

It lost its InterCity services in the 1990s and is now served by Silverlink trains on the Euston - Northampton service as the main line trains go thundering through at high speed.

The Bedford branch happily survives and it has had its signalling recently modernised and is in prospect of an increase of speed limit. But the loss of lines west and local branch lines worked from Bletchley has reduced its status a great deal. The goods yard is still in use for the storage and shipment of building stone.

About to enter on the Bletchley shed turntable the Ivatt Mogul no M3003. Although it is not apparent in the photograph, this is a new locomotive, one of twenty M3000-M3019 delivered to the system in 1947. It is seen here on April 10, 1948. They were classified as 4F freight engines and numbered 162 in class, the prefix 'M' was soon dispensed with.

H C Casserley

Bletchley shed in the steam and sulpherous vapours that had some atmospheric endearment to lovers of steam locomotives. In its midst two engines, the farther being a 3F 0-6-0 goods engine no 3419 and the Black Five 4968 still in its LMS livery as this is still only April 10, 1948.

H C Casserley

The age of electrification, a 'Britannia' class speeds towards Bletchley from the south. On the left distance can be seen the chimneys of the Bletchley brickworks with the buffer stops for its sidings in front of the hut. Looking at marks in the ground it appears that this siding was connected through an 'up' side turnout to another line close to the train. The brickworks began production in 1934.

Andrew Bratton

Standing on the line that had for so many years received trains from Oxford one of the former LNWR 0-6-2 tanks no 6883. The tank version of the largely utilised 18" Goods 0-6-0 called 'Cauliflowers'. This was on February 11, 1948, the engine was withdrawn three months later after forty-nine years in harness. The view also provides some appreciation of the superb LNWR station buildings including a hotel.

H C Casserley

One of the Webb 'Coal Tanks' on the Bletchley wheel drop having had the front driving wheel set removed. August 22, 1948.

H C Casserley

Arriving from the north, 'Jubilee' 4-6-0 no 5586 'Mysore' with the 8.00 am Liverpool - Euston express. Bletchley shed lines on the left.

H C Casserley

A 'Coal Tank' with some longevity, no 27830 was introduced in 1896. It received an LMS number in 1927 and took a British Railways number 58934 before it was scrapped in October 1949.

H C Casserley

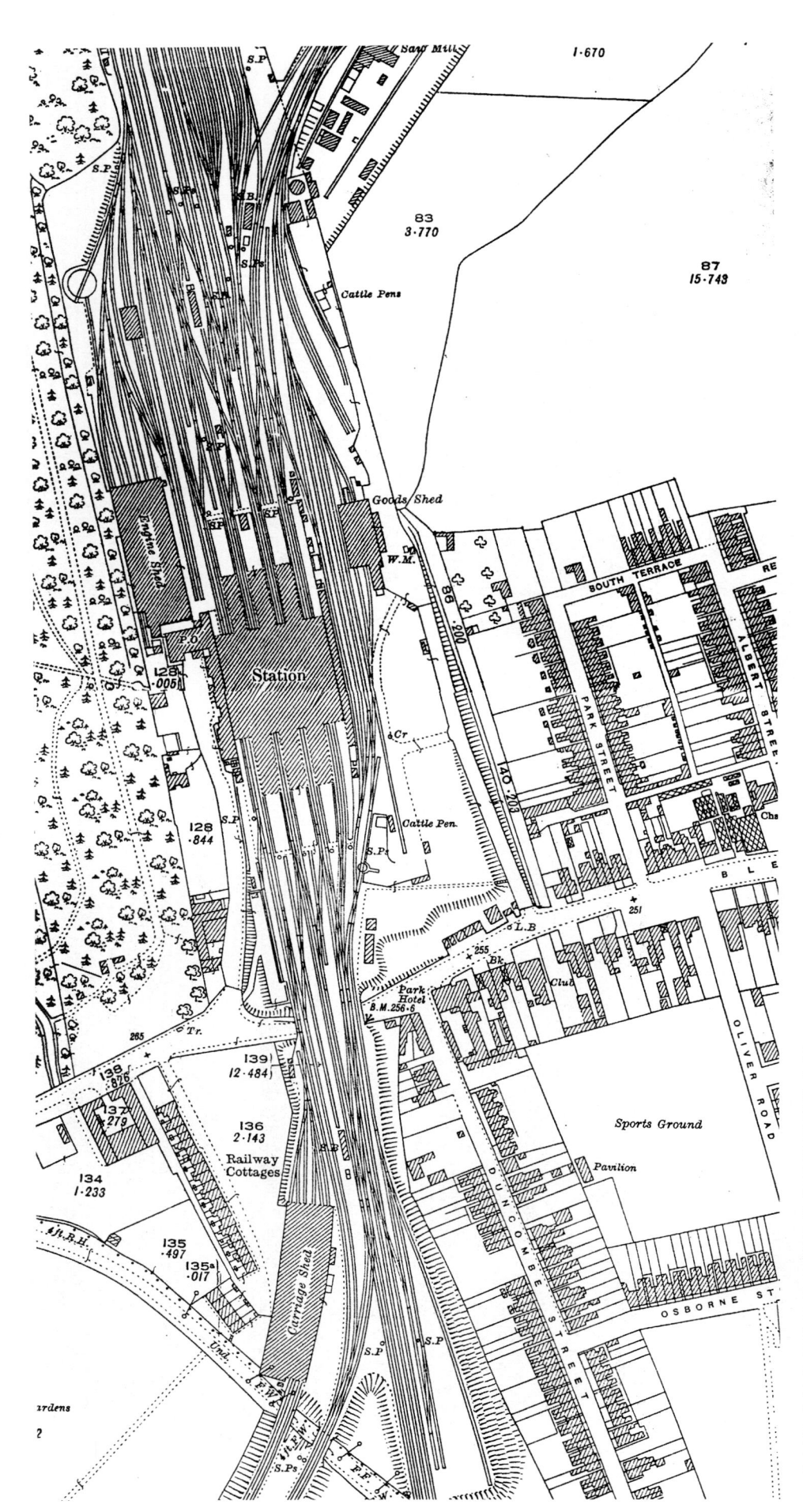

Bletchley station in the 1930s under LMS ownership. This is probably its most complete form. Even the old London & Birmingham water tank house has not yet been demolished. See the hatched square immediately in front of the station entrance. Note also the small turnplate near the cattle dock. All of the housing close to the station accommodated the considerable number of staff employed at the station, which at its peak went to 600. Combining this with the railway works town of Wolverton a few miles north shows how much the employment and the economy of north Buckinghamshire was dependant upon the railway.
Ordnance Survey

The old 'Worcester' curve used in 1853 to allow a connection for through trains avoiding Bletchley station to join north of Oxford with the Oxford, Wocester & Wolverhampton Railway. It was removed some time in the later nineteenth century. Fortuitously with the completion of the Bletchley Brick Company factory in 1934 a siding to the new brickworks utilised the space of the former through line. The above photograph shows the connection onto the Oxford - Bletchley line with the headshunt alongside. A new signalbox was built of the Midland/LMS pattern called 'Fletton's Sidings'.

D S Barrie

So much for the rule on black smoke in stations! That aside this does give a good view of Bletchley largly intact, the hotel on the left and the LNWR all-over roof. As th era of steam recedes from memory such views are very evocative of the time. The very tall signals of the LNWR that allowed 'up' trains to site them for some distance travelling south are cut off in this photograph.

H C Casserley

This handbill supersedes
CLA 75

C/LA83

DIESEL TRAIN SERVICE

BETWEEN
BLETCHLEY—BUCKINGHAM and BANBURY (MERTON STREET)

12th SEPTEMBER 1960 and until further notice

WEEKDAYS ONLY

	D am	D am	D am	D am	am	am	D pm	SX pm	SX pm	SO pm	SO pm	D pm	B pm	pm	D pm	D SO pm
BLETCHLEY .. .. dep.	5 20	7 10	7 55	9 15	..	11 39	12 30	1 55	..	..	2 5	..	3 40	..	5 28	9 5
SWANBOURNE .. ,,	..	7 20	8 4	9 25	..	11 49	12 39	2 5	..	..	2 15	..	3 50	..	5 38	9 14
WINSLOW .. .. ,,	..	7 25	8 8	9 30	..	11 54	12 43	2 10	..	..	2 20	..	3 55	..	5 44	9 18
VERNEY JUNCTION .. ,,	..	7 30	8 12	9 35	..	11 59	12 47	2 15	..	..	2 25	..	4 0	..	5 49	9 22
PADBURY .. .. ,,	..	7 35	8 17	9 40	..	12 4	12 52	2 20	..	..	2 30	..	4 5	..	5 54	9 27
BUCKINGHAM .. arr.	5 40	7 41	8 22	9 46	..	12 10	12 57	2 26	..	..	2 36	..	4 11	..	6 0	9 32
BUCKINGHAM .. dep.	5 49	..	8 25	..	10 0	..	12 57	..	2 30	..	2 40	..	4 30	..	6 30	9 32
RADCLIVE HALT .. ,,	..	..	8 27	..	10 2	..	12 59	..	2 32	..	2 42	..	4 32	..	6 32	9 34
WATER STRATFORD HALT ,,	..	..	8 31	..	10 6	..	1 2	..	2 36	..	2 46	..	4 36	..	6 36	9 38
FULWELL & WESTBURY .. ,,	5 56	..	8 35	..	10 10	..	1 6	..	2 40	..	2 50	..	4 40	..	6 40	9 42
BRACKLEY .. .. ,,	6A 8	..	8 40	..	10 15	..	1 12	..	2 45	..	2 55	..	4 45	..	6 45	9 47
BANBURY (Merton Street) .. arr.	6 21	..	8 54	..	10 29	..	1 26	..	2 59	..	3 9	..	4 59	..	6 59	10 1

	D am	D am	D am	am	D am	pm	D pm	SX pm	SO pm	D pm	D pm	pm	D pm	D SO pm
BANBURY (Merton Street) .. dep.	6 50	..	9 16	..	10 45	..	1 55	..	..	3 45	..	5 50	..	7 14	..	10 15
BRACKLEY .. .. ,,	7 3	..	9 30	..	10 58	..	2 8	..	..	3 58	..	6 3	..	7 28	..	10 27
FULWELL & WESTBURY .. ,,	7 8	..	9 35	..	11 3	..	2 13	..	..	4 3	..	6 8	..	7 33	..	10 33
WATER STRATFORD HALT ,,	7 12	..	9 39	..	11 7	..	2 17	..	..	4 7	..	6 12	..	7 37	..	10 37
RADCLIVE HALT .. ,,	7 16	..	9 42	..	11 11	..	2 21	..	..	4 11	..	6 16	..	7 40	..	10 41
BUCKINGHAM .. arr.	7 19	..	9 46	..	11 13	..	2 24	..	..	4 14	..	6 19	..	7 44	..	10 44
BUCKINGHAM .. dep.	7 20	7 50	..	9 51	11 14	12 20	..	2 35	2 45	..	4 21	..	6 36	7 45	..	10 45
PADBURY .. .. ,,	7 23	7 54	..	9 56	11 18	12 24	..	2 39	2 49	..	4 25	..	6 40	7 48	..	10 48
VERNEY JUNCTION .. ,,	7 28	8 0	..	10 0	11 23	12 29	..	2 44	2 54	..	4 30	..	6 46	7 53	..	10 53
WINSLOW .. .. ,,	7 33	8 6	..	10 6	11 27	12 35	..	2 50	3 0	..	4 36	..	6 52	7 58	..	10 58
SWANBOURNE .. ,,	7 37	8 11	..	10 11	11 32	12 40	..	2 55	3 5	..	4 41	..	6 57	8 3	..	11 2
BLETCHLEY .. arr.	7 46	8 21	..	10 20	11 41	12 50	..	3 5	3 15	..	4 51	..	7 7	8 11	..	11 11

NOTES :—A—Arrives Brackley at 6.3 a.m. **B**—On and from 21st Nov. 1960 this train will run 4 minutes later throughout
D—Diesel Rail Car. Second Class only   **SO**—Saturdays only   **SX**—Saturdays excepted.

Published by British Railways (L.M.Region)
C/LA83 October 1960

BRITISH RAILWAYS

B.R. 35000 Staffords, Netherfield

The last timetable to be printed for passenger services over the Buckingham—Banbury (Merton Street) branch, where passenger service ceased on Sat. 31 December, 1960 with the 10.15pm from Banbury.

Andrew Bratton Collection

Bletchley seen at what could be regarded as the high point of the station and the workings of the Oxford - Cambridge lines around 1900. The suggestion is that a 'Lady of the Lake' or 'Problem' class is about to be piloted from Bletchley on an Oxford line train by a 5ft 6 in 2-4-2 tank travelling bunker first.

R M Casserley Collection

One of the diesel railcars in no 2 platform at Bletchley with the 10.46 to Buckingham on Friday, September 7, 1962. It is just before electrification required the removal of the all over roof and no 1 platform on the left was filled-in with no 2 platform being reduced to north and south bays.

Andrew Bratton

A dark time for the nation apart from the icy grip on defunct locomotives on Bletchley shed. As this is January 29, 1940 the summer of greatest trial lay ahead.

H C Casserley

The station prepared for the beginning of the daily timetable with both passenger train coach sets in the sidings on the right.
Bill Simpson

Rewley Road - The Model

Members of the Oxford and District Model Railway Club completed a superb model of Radley station on the former Great Western line from Oxford to Didcot in the early 1970's. This was, for a time, the club layout.

They then looked around for a local club project to undertake, being interested in recording the local scene in model form.

At that time there were still quite few remnants of post Beeching sites of stations surviving in Oxfordshire, but they had just completed a country station and wanted to move forward with something more ambitious.

The Oxford GWR station would make demands of space and time beyond realistic possibility but it was decided that the terminus station alongside, the ex LNWR/LMS station was a possibility and would give plenty of scope for variety in train working, whereas Radley simply had trains running through with interest being supplied by the working of the Abingdon branch.

With the help of the club chairman Colin Judge of Oxford Publishing Co many plans were acquired and after some study eyebrows were raised at the prospect of just what was to be undertaken. It was going to call on dedication and stamina in spadefuls, but a determined group was formed and preliminary work was undertaken. Survey groups went to the site to photograph and measure what was still visible. The station building was being used by a tyre supply company, whilst the coal yard was still in use. Also the swingbridge was more or less permanently across the canal with the point rodding frame still fixed to it. A demonstration of the movement of the bridge was presented to a group of enthusiasts in 1981 by British Railways Western Region.

In terms of modelling it is fair to point out that in the early 1970's materials and techniques for scratch building scale models were not as plentiful as nowadays.

Using measurements on site, photographs and scale plans a number of drawings were made, luckily draughtsmanship skills were available in the group.

The group assembled behind the layout at the special display at the Buckinghamshire Railway Centre to celebrate the opening of the restored station that had been brought from Oxford. A rare occasion indeed when a model ran running to timetable on the platform of the original! From left to right Alan Sollis, Jim Briggs, John Warren, Brian Garland, Martin Byles, Dave Potter, Richard Gardiner.

Bill Simpson

The layout operating during the occasion referred to above. On the extreme left a stalwart not included on the group picture - Ron Alcock.

Bill Simpson

Looking across the layout from a position that in actual life would be the site of the GWR station. Note the working wagon turnplate on the right. One of the ingenious mechanisms designed and built by Brian Garland.

Bill Simpson

The drawings of separate structures were then allocated to members to work on.

The triumph of Rewley Road was the way that this was undertaken with a long term view. Most people enjoy the adrenaline rush of an idea and model railway clubs are like most other societies in this. But all successful creative work needs a reservoir of continuous energy and solid idealism to maintain a long haul. The prospect of pride and satisfaction in the achievement being some way beyond the horizon. For now it would be sheer dogged determined progress, like digging a tunnel.

It has to be borne in mind also that to run the layout in the selected dateline of c1935, most of the locomotives and stock would have to be scratchbuilt!

Rewley Road was first exhibited as a complete layout on October 23, 1976 at the Watford model railway exhibition. Before then it had appeared at the Oxford show in the Town Hall in various stages of progress from 1972. After completion the layout has been exhibited thirty seven times at various locations from York in the north to Southampton in the south. Apart from the addition of an engineering train the same sequence of trains has been retained, although the stock now more closely reflects the LNWR origins of the railway. As the layout neared completion a brilliant but demanding decision was made. This was to follow work pioneered by Oxford Club members Les Eden (Bossington) in 1968 and John Pomroy (Winton). They compiled a sequence of trains making use of timetables of the period and used a recorded commentary. This was undertaken on Rewley Road covering all the aspects of the site. It had two important results, to provide information for viewers and to concentrate the minds of the operators.

Running the correct trains on a scale model would be appreciated by enthusiasts with a keen sense of history, but much would be lost to the general public at exhibitions, so the commentary explained what was happening. As described, this took the layout and its operation into another dimension where operators could not simply twiddle knobs and recalcitrant trains be given a quick furtive push. It had to operate with a perfection unlikely even in real life and the operators had to give the running of the 45 minute session 100% concentration. Often the intrigued public would ask questions over the layout during operation and would be ignored,

A view from over the swingbridge looking back towards the station buildings. Delicate models like signals and the crane of Axtell, Perry on the left make transporting the layout to exhibitions a concentrated and time consuming business which is secured by the dedication of the group. The locomotive taking out the express to Bletchley is a 4-6-0 unrebuilt member of the LMS 'Patriot' class named 'Isle of Man' no 5511. A class with an odd assembly of names inherited from the LNWR, including recognition of patriotism from the First World War then continued further to include favourite seaside locations and the famous railway timetable compiler 'Bradshaw'. It will be noted from this view in the mid 1970s that the model staithes on the coal yard sidings have not yet been made.

B H Higgins

something that the operators were very embarrassed about. But they literally could not stop thinking of what they were doing. So it was decided to announce time available at the end of the session for all questions.

In the thirty years or so that the layout has represented Oxford in many parts of the United Kingdom, it has been received with delight and fascination. The operators have always felt that their efforts were well rewarded by the appreciation expressed by the thousands that have watched its timetable progress through the compressed day.

Regrettably, over such a long timespan of thirty years the layout has been visited by tragedy. The deaths of of John Warren in 2002 and Jim Briggs in 2004 were not only a great loss to their families and friends but also their roles as core members of the group. Fortunately others came forward to learn operations. But their personalities and the dedicated work that they did was a permanent loss. As their stock is still run on the layout it helps the group to feel that they are still a part of the operation.

It is difficult to be precise about for how long Rewley Road will remain available, all things are finite and the ageing group find that moving the heavy boards around cannot be done so nimbly as it was. Therefore this chapter is intended to ensure that it will never be forgotten so that an important transport feature of the City of Oxford can be read about when its subject is no longer surviving both in real life and the model that so vividly expressed it.

Alan Sollis

One of the operators of the Rewley Road model, Alan Sollis, has a particular interest, in it. He was a boy telegraph clerk in the GWR north station signalbox. This box was almost back to back with the LNWR signalbox. Alan worked in the GWR box period 1950-3, so he witnessed the final days of the passenger service into Rewley Road before it was transferred over to the north bays of the GWR station.

As a young lad of seventeen he had a particular interest in waving to office girls arriving to work on the line as carriage windows glided by beneath the box.

He also had an opportunity to witness the operation of the swingbridge, as once a week a narrow boat loaded with spoil would come down the Oxford Canal to access the Thames. Two men would then come walking up from the station and commence the process of turning the handles geared to the pivot, slowly swinging it clear for the canal.

He recalled one working from Swanbourne Goods Yard that left there at 3.30 am. It moved in rather dilatory fashion behind an ex LNWR 0-8-0 'Super D'. Looking back there is something slightly romantic in this lone engine slogging its slow progress through the countryside at night. But it would not be seen that way by the crossing keepers opening and closing the gates behind it with a big yawn. Eventually it would thread its way across Oxford North Junction onto the GWR heading for Hinksey Yard. It trundled through the GWR station centre road with its long train seeming to take forever in the section. The relief of getting rid of it was short lived. For as soon as it had deposited its train it needed to come back through the station to turn on Oxford shed turntable. It then went back to Hinksey to pick up another train to do its journey in reverse. All the moving around was at the height of the Oxford morning rush hour so it was by no means a welcome guest.

It was with mixed feelings, as a lover of steam locomotives, when he saw for the first time a brand new shiny green diesel come from Swanbourne with the same train carrying out the entire operation in half the time needing only to drop off, pick up, and go back, clearing the station much earlier.

The passenger service at that time was in the charge of 2-6-4 Stanier and Fairburn tank engines which were displaced by British Railways 2-6-4 Standard tanks. The only unusual engine of the day would be the visiting D16 4-4-0 tender engine from Cambridge that brought in the late morning passenger and returned at 2.28 pm.

In 1947 an LMS 4-4-0 came to grief in the coal yard where he saw it lying on its side. This kind of thing happened most often on semi derelict lines were wartime astringency had prevented replacement of rotting sleepers.

Railway Modellers Cup for Layout of the Year 1976

The following is a list of exhibition venues that Rewley Road has visited in its long history and is therefore probably unique.

1	Watford	Oct 23, 1976
2	Oxford	Nov 20, 1976
3	York	Apr 9-11-12 1977 3 days)
4	Salisbury	May 14, 1977
5	Abingdon	June 4, 1977
6	Leamington	Oct 15, 1977
7	Oxford	Nov 26, 1977
8	York	Easter 1978 (3 days)
9	Southampton	April 22, 1978
10	Heml Hempstd	Sept 23, 1978
11	Warley	Oct 7, 8, 1978
12	Wolverhampton	May 5, 6, 7, 1979
13	Abingdon	June 9, 1979
14	Kidlington	August 24, 1979
15	Coventry	Sept 29, 1979
16	Milton Keynes	Nov 10, 1979
17	Enfield	Dec 1, 1979
18	Kettering	Sept 20, 1980
19	Wheatley	Oct, 1980
20	Oxford	Nov, 1980
21	Leamington	Oct 24, 1981
22	Watford	Oct 16, 1983
23	Oxford	Nov, 1983
24	Swindon	Nov, 1983 (2 day)
25	Didcot	Sept, 1984
26	Kidlington	Jan, 1985 (2 day)
27	Aylesbury	Oct 5, 1985
28	Stoneleigh	Aug 1986 (3 day)
29	Oxford	Oct 17, 19, 1987 (2 day)
30	St Albans	Jan 13, 14, 1990 (2 day)
		Chiltern Model Railway Association 25 years
31	Biggleswade	Feb 10, 1990
		East Bedfordshire Club
32	Oxford	Oct 13, 1990
		Oxford Club 25 Years Anniversary Exhibition
33	Oxford	Oct 26, 1996
34	Quainton	May 2001 (3 day) Bank Holiday
		Buckinghamshire Railway Centre
35	Quainton	May 2002 (3 day) Bank Holiday
		Buckinghamshire Railway Centre
36	Cheltenham	Oct 2004 (2 day)
37	Wantage	Oct 15, 2005
38	Oxford	Sept 30, 2006
		Risinghurst School, Headington

The London & North Western Railway is well represented on the layout even though it is set in the 1930s. The Engineers' Train is hauled by an 18" Goods or Cauliflower, the original 8367 was withdrawn in November 1947. The last '18" Goods' engine of the LNWR to be condemned was no 58427. This was at Trafford Park, Manchester, it was withdrawn in December 1955. In this view the train is crossing the swingbridge to the distraction of a college swell who must have made some impression on his lady friend, having punted from Folly Bridge!

Andrew Burchett

The '18" Goods' seen with the Engineers' Train crossing the bridge from another angle.

Andrew Burchett

Although somewhat derelict what did survive of the station was very welcome in 1980 when these photographs were taken. The Stationmaster's house is a good example as a working drawing was made from the building extant.

Oxford Model Railway Club

The late Jim Briggs took up the challenge of making this building and the superb result is his legacy on the layout. Here Jim is seen holding a surveyor's pole to help with measurements.

Oxford Model Railway Club

91

Jim holds the measuring pole in front of the row of Coal Offices that were on Rewley Road.
Oxford Model Railway Club

Member Martin Byles spent many hours in studied contemplation to create realistic atitudes and situations for the dumb impassive model people that will never board the trains, but must look as if they are filled with determination to do so!
Andrew Burchett

At macro photographic dimensions it is possible to create the illusion of being 25 millimeters high!
Andrew Burchett

The steam shed was faithfully modelled including its distinctive water tower.

Andrew Burchett

One of the features designed and built by Brian Garland ingeniously re-creates a feature often overlooked, that much work in yards was done by man and horse. The figure standing on the rail moves forward and using a pinch bar pushing the wagon a few scale feet onto the wagon turnplate. The plate is motorised and turns the wagon 45 degrees to reconnect with its train. As this feature is at the front of the layout and at the eye level of young people it is viewed with delight mixed with incredulity!

Andrew Burchett

Men working on permanent way work, superb detail suggesting animated movement.

Andrew Burchett

Only one of the passenger rakes is in position on its siding which suggests the timetable is in mid progression. The glow of station lamps does much to create atmosphere.

Andrew Burchett

All the feeling of a bustling goods yard is re-created with people busily pre-occupied.

Andrew Burchett

Jim seriously ensured that the kitchen garden of the Stationmaster's house would be well represented with copious detail.
Andrew Burchett

An aerial view of the Goods yard showing the distribution of buildings and vehicles.
Andrew Burchett

Collecting data, the author miniscule, crouched over writing paper in the far corner of the bridge, oblivious to the GWR box and signal gantry behind.

Oxford Model Railway Club

They could be dicussing the major spectacle of the year, the burning down of the Crystal Palace. Or the magnificent triumph of Fred Perry at Wimbledon the year before.

Andrew Burchett